Cooking on the Move

This book

was presented to the

ACC

William J. Spangler Library

by

Zack Hanle

PHOTO CREDIT
The cover photo shows a Hinckley Sou'wester 42 under sail. Reproduced
by permission of Henry R. Hinckley & Company, Southwest Harbor,
Maine, U.S.A.

Library of Congress Cataloging in Publication Data

Gingell, Rika.
   Cooking on the move.

   1. Cookery. 2. Cookery, Marine. 3. Mobile home living. I. title.
TX652.G56 1983 641.5'75 82-19057
ISBN 0-88427-052-1

Manufactured in the United States of America

CONTENTS

Dedication

To my husband Roy, who survived all my cooking experiments in rough seas and calm weather, and who still wants me as crew.

R.G.

Preface

This cookbook is the result of years of perfecting recipes that can be baked in a small space. It came into existence while we were cruising the tropical waters of the South Pacific in our sailboat *Honnalee*. Baking bread every three days, for example, caused oven heat that when added to the tropical temperatures, made the boat unbearable.

"Why not bake on the top of the stove?" I asked myself.

Experimenting first with bread recipes, and using a saucepan and asbestos pad to control the heat of the primus burner, I finally succeeded in learning how to bake the lightest loaves of golden-brown bread on the top of the stove.

The small heating area of the saucepan was more economical than heating an oven, so I proceeded to adjust other favorite recipes from all over the world to respond to ths method of baking. Deep rich chocolate cakes, light fluffy sponges, mouth-watering pies, and delicious dishes made from recipes from the South Pacific to the Mediterranean flowed from my tiny kitchen—all fit to grace any table, and all baked or cooked on the top of my tiny galley stove.

During the ninety-thousand miles my husband and I have sailed, I have continued to improve and simplify this method of baking and cooking. My original intention was to write a sailing cookbook, but I have since discovered that there are thousands of people from all walks of life, who have a limited area in which to cook, and who also appreciate a cooler kitchen.

There is no need to go without your delicacies or sweets anymore. *Cooking on the Move* explains how to bake on one burner. The speed and simplicity of this method is a delightful experience.

All of the recipes that follow are tested, economical, and easy to prepare.

I hope you find as much enjoyment in using this collection as I have had in producing it for you.

RIKA GINGELL

Utensils for Stove-Top Baking and Cooking

You will need the following basic utensils:

Heavy Aluminum Saucepan

This should have a one-quarter inch vent in the lid. The base should be approximately 8 inches in diameter. The ideal is a pressure cooker without a gauge. However, if you use a saucepan and it does not have a vent in the lid, have one drilled in the center. Here are some of the things you can do with the saucepan: bake cakes and breads, deep-fat fry, roast meat, bake potatoes, and cook pasta, chowders and soups. I discovered a bonus feature: nothing slops over the side of the pan when the sea is rough!

Aluminum Non-Stick Skillet

The base of this pan should be about 7 inches in diameter, and you will not need one with a lid. This utensil will be useful for baking pie shells and cookies, for small quantity frying, and for making pizza.

Heavy Cast Iron Skillet with a Lid

This will be used for cooking casserole-type dishes, to make pizza, to bake fish, and to make skillet breads, Chinese dishes, crepes, pancakes and cookies.

Small Saucepan with Lid

Use this pan for cooking vegetables, rice, sauces and pie fillings.

Asbestos Pad

This pad should be 5 by 5 inches, and it must be one-quarter inch thick. Have six holes drilled through at random. This makes the pad heat more evenly. CAUTION: Do *not* use an asbestos shingle. Some of these explode when hot.

Hints for Coping When You Don't Have Required Ingredients

Milk

If fresh milk isn't available, as it often is not when you are sailing or camping, use canned evaporated milk diluted with an equal amount of water or powdered milk mixed according to the directions on the package.

Cream

Use undiluted canned evaporated milk, or dilute it and then add more powdered milk than called for in the instructions.

Sour Cream

There are two ways to make sour cream substitute: Add lemon juice to a can of evaporated milk, *or* mix three-quarters of a small can of evaporated milk with two scant, tablespoons of vinegar. This last method is called "jury-rig sour cream."

Stock

Use beef, chicken, fish, or vegetable bouillon cubes or packets dissolved in hot water to make quick stock. Canned chicken broth or stock is also available.

Herbs

Onions, chili, parsley, basil, oregano, garlic, and many other herbs are available in dehydrated form. When you use them, add a little extra water to achieve the same consistency as fresh seasoning.

Fruits

Canned or fresh fruits can be used for most sauces and pie fillings. Substitute the syrup from the canned fruits for the sugar or water called for in the recipe.

A Simple
Metric Conversion Table

The equivalents and conversions given here are applicable to kitchen use.
The capacity of cups and spoons and the volume of their contents may be measured in liters or parts of a liter.

"MI" stands for milliliter, and there are 1000 milliliters in a liter.

1/4 cup = 60 ml, or 4 tablespoons
1/2 cup = 125 ml
1 cup = 250 ml
4 cups = 1000 ml, or 1 liter
1 liter = 1 3/4 pints
4 liters = 7 pints
4 1/2 liters = 1 gallon

The recipes in this book are based on the above volume sizes. The teaspoons and tablespoons used are the conventional kitchen teaspoons and tablespoons. All measurements are for level teaspoons and tablespoons, unless otherwise stated in a recipe.

Baking

BREADS

Instructions for Making Yeast Breads

1. After the dough has been well-kneaded, shape it into a ball.
2. Oil the bottom and sides of a heavy saucepan. Put the dough into the saucepan and turn it over to oil all its sides. Put on the lid and set pan in a warm spot for about 1 hour or until it has doubled in bulk.
3. When dough has risen light the stove and set the asbestos pad over a high flame. Put the saucepan on the pad, and when the lid is too hot to touch, turn the heat down to medium-low and cook bread for 25-30 minutes.
4. Tap the top of the loaf: if it sounds hollow, the bread is done.
5. Put a rack across the top of the saucepan and turn the bread out. It should slide out of the pan easily.
6. If you want the top browned, turn the bread over and return to the saucepan. Put on back of the stove and cook for another 5-7 minutes until brown.
7. Turn the bread onto a rack and let it cool before cutting. These recipes make a loaf about 8 inches in diameter and 4 inches high.

Top-of-the-Stove Yeast Bread

INGREDIENTS

3/4	Tsp	Salt
3	Cups	Flour
		Water
		Sugar
1	Tbl or pkt	Dried yeast
3	Tbls	Shortening, margarine, or butter

DIRECTIONS

Put 1 teaspoon sugar and warm water in small bowl and mix in dried yeast. Set aside in a warm place until yeast begins to work.

Pour slightly more than 1 cup of boiling water into another bowl. Add shortening, salt, and 1 tablespoon sugar. Mix well and set aside to cool to lukewarm.

While the yeast is working and the water cooling, sift flour into a large mixing bowl. When the yeast has bubbled, add it to the center of the flour and stir to a thin paste. Add the lukewarm water slowly and keep stirring until dough is too stiff to handle with a spoon. Turn it onto a floured breadboard and knead for at least 5 minutes; this is important as it determines the texture of the bread. Form dough into a ball.

Follow instructions for cooking yeast breads, page 1.

Easy Yeast Coffee Cake
Mix night before and cook in the morning for breakfast.

INGREDIENTS

1/2	Cup	Milk
2	Cups	Flour
1	Tbl	Sugar
1		Egg
1	Tsp	Salt
1	Tbl	Dried yeast
1/2	Cup	Butter

(continued)

DIRECTIONS

Cut the butter into the flour and add salt. Beat the egg slightly. Warm the
milk, add the egg, sugar, and yeast, and beat in the flour. Let stand for
about 3 hours. Stir down and put into a well-oiled saucepan. Put the lid on
and let stand overnight.

In the morning following the instructions for making yeast breads, page 1.
When the coffee cake has cooled, cover it with confectioners sugar mixed
with enough water to make a stiff paste. Top with nuts or chopped dried fruits.

Oatmeal Honey Yeast Bread
Honey gives this bread a different flavor

INGREDIENTS

1/2	Cup	Warm water
1	Tsp	Sugar
1	Tbl	Dried yeast
1	Cup	Sour milk
1/4	Tsp	Baking soda
3	Tbls	Liquid honey
1	Tsp	Salt
1	Cup	Quick cooking oats
2 1/3	Cups	White flour

DIRECTIONS

Combine the warm water, sugar, and yeast in a mixing bowl; stir and let
stand 10 minutes.

Heat the sour milk until lukewarm, remove from heat, and add baking soda,
salt, honey, and oats. Add the yeast mixture and 1 cup sifted flour. Beat
well and add 1/2 cup flour. Knead the remaining flour into the dough until
the dough is smooth; this takes about 5 minutes. You can let the dough
rise to double its bulk and then knead again or just knead once.

Follow instructions for making yeast breads, page 1.

White Batter Yeast Bread

INGREDIENTS

4	Cups	White flour, unsifted
3	Tbls	Sugar
1	Tsp	Salt
2	Packages	Dried yeast
1	Cup	Milk
1	Cup	Water
2	Tbls	Margarine

DIRECTIONS

Mix 1 1/2 cups flour, and salt in a large bowl. Heat milk and water and pour 1/4 cup into a small bowl; when lukewarm add the yeast and 1 teaspoon sugar. Set aside to bubble.

Add the margarine to the remaining milk. When melted, set aside to cool to lukewarm.

Gradually add the yeast mixture to 1 1/2 cups of flour and other dry ingredients to make a thin paste. Add the warm milk and beat well until the batter is smooth. Add 1 more cup of flour to make a stiff batter. Beat until well-blended. Cover and let rise in a warm place until it has doubled its bulk about 40 minutes. Stir the batter down and beat vigorously for about half a minute.

Follow instructions for making yeast breads, page 1. This bread should cook for about 40 minutes.

Instructions For Making Baking Powder Breads

1. All baking powder breads must be cooked in a hot saucepan to get a light, fluffy texture.

2. Oil the saucepan with 1/2 to 1 tablespoon of oil.

3. Light the burner and turn it up to high heat. Put the asbestos pad on top of the flame and place the oiled saucepan on top of it. Start to make the baking powder bread.

4. When the saucepan lid is too hot to touch, turn the burner down. The pan is now ready for the bread.

5. Put the bread into the saucepan and put the lid on.

6. Cook for approximately 30 minutes unless the recipe states otherwise.

7. When the bread is cooked, it makes a hollow sound when tapped on the top.

8. Turn the bread onto a rack to cool.

Boston Brown Bread

INGREDIENTS

1	Cup	Whole wheat or graham flour
1	Cup	Cornmeal
1	Cup	Ground, rolled oats
5	Tsp	Baking powder
1	Tsp	Salt
3/4	Cup	Molasses
1 1/3	Cups	Milk

DIRECTIONS

Mix the dry ingredients thoroughly. Add molasses to the milk and when it is dissolved, add to the dry ingredients. Beat thoroughly and put into a well-oiled saucepan.

Follow instructions for cooking baking powder breads, page 4. Cook over low heat for 1 1/2 hours.

Steamed Boston Brown Bread

INGREDIENTS

2/3	Cup	All-purpose flour
2/3	Cup	Yellow cornmeal
2/3	Cup	Whole wheat flour
3/4	Tsp	Salt
3/4	Tsp	Baking soda
1/2	Cup	Molasses
1	Cup	Buttermilk

DIRECTIONS

Sift all-purpose flour, cornmeal, and whole wheat flour with salt and soda. Mix molasses and buttermilk together, stir well, and pour over the mixed dried ingredients. Beat until smooth and pour into a well-greased pudding bowl.

Cover tightly and put on a trivet in a saucepan or deep kettle. Add boiling water to the saucepan until it comes halfway up the sides of the bowl. Cover with lid and steam approximately 3 hours. Check occasionally to see if more water needs be added.

Breakfast Loaf

INGREDIENTS

4	Cups	Flour
1/2	Cup	Sugar
3/4	Tsp	Salt
2	Tbls	Baking powder
1	Cup	Milk
4		Eggs
1 1/2	Tbls	Sugar

DIRECTIONS

Sift together several times the flour, sugar, salt, and baking powder. Beat the eggs, add milk and then melted shortening. Combine the mixtures and knead on a floured board for 5 minutes. Place dough in an oiled saucepan, put in a warm place, and allow it to rise for 1 hour with lid on.

Put the saucepan on a hot asbestos pad and turn flame down to medium when lid is too hot to touch. Cook for 30 minutes, but if not done, leave on burner until it sounds hollow when tapped.

Brown Health Bread

INGREDIENTS

2	Cups	Wholemeal flour
2	Tsps	Baking powder
1/2	Tsp	Salt
1	Tbl	Butter (heaping)
1	Cup	each of, raisins, chopped dates, and nuts
1	Scant Tbl	Corn syrup
1	Cup	Boiling water
1/2	Cup	Milk

DIRECTIONS

Mix flour, baking powder, and salt together. Rub in butter and add dates, raisins, and nuts. Add milk and syrup to boiling water and mix with the dry ingredients.

Prepare the saucepan as directed on page 4. Pour the batter into the saucepan and cook covered over low to medium heat for 45-50 minutes.

Honnalee's Corn Bread

INGREDIENTS

1	Cup	Flour
1	Cup	Yellow cornmeal
3/4	Tsp	Salt
1/2	Cup	Granulated sugar
4	Tsps	Baking Powder
1	Cup	+2 Tbls Milk
4	Tbls	Oil or shortening
1		Egg

DIRECTIONS

Sift flour and mix it with the other dry ingredients in a large bowl. Add milk and egg and beat for 1 minute. Add cooking oil or shortening and beat for another minute.

Follow instructions on page 4. Cook over medium heat for 25 minutes or until the top springs back when touched. Serve hot with butter.

Easy Baking Powder Bread

INGREDIENTS

2	Cups	Flour
1	Tbl	Sugar
1/2	Tsp	Salt
2	Tsp	Baking powder
1	Tbl	Margarine or shortening
		Water as needed

DIRECTIONS

Sift flour and mix with other dry ingredients. These can be prepared ahead of time and stored in a jar so they will be ready for use when sailing, camping, or on busy days.

When ready to use, pour mixture into a bowl and cut in margarine or shortening. Add enough water to make a stiff but sticky dough. Follow instructions for making baking powder breads, page 4.

Cornmeal Bread

INGREDIENTS

2	Cups	Flour
1	Cup	Cornmeal
1/2	Tsp	Salt
4	Tsps	Baking powder
3	Tbls	Oil
1	Tsp	Powdered milk
1	Cup	Water

DIRECTIONS

Mix the flour, cornmeal, salt, and baking powder together. Dripple the oil over the dry mixture and stir to blend well. Add powdered milk to the water and pour over dry ingredients. Turn the dough onto a floured board and knead for a few seconds. Shape into a round and put into an oiled saucepan and cook over medium heat for 30-40 minutes. Follow directions for cooking baking powder breads, page 4.

VARIATION

You can make hominy grit bread by substituting 1 cup of hominy grits for the cornmeal in this recipe.

Oatmeal Baking Powder Bread

INGREDIENTS

1	Cup	Flour
1	Cup	Oatmeal
1/2	Tsp	Salt
1/2	Tsp	Powdered milk
1/2	Tsp	Sugar
1	Tsp	Baking powder for every cup of water used

DIRECTIONS

Mix the above ingredients together with water until you have a stiff dough. Knead as little as possible. Follow directions on page 4. Cook 20-30 minutes.

Potato Bread
A mashed cold boiled potato is used

INGREDIENTS

2	Cups	Flour
1/2	Tsp	Salt
1/2	Tsp	Sugar
3	Tsps	Baking powder
1/2		Medium sized cold, boiled potato
		Milk or water as needed

DIRECTIONS

Mix the flour, salt, sugar, and baking powder in a bowl. Rub the potato through a sieve or mash finely and add to the flour mixture. Add enough milk or water to make a stiff but sticky batter. Place at once in a warmed, oiled saucepan. Smooth the top with a spoon dipped in butter and stand in a warm, draft-free place for 30 minutes.

Then follow the instructions on page 4 and cook for 30 minutes.

Raisin Bread

INGREDIENTS

2	Cups	Flour
1/2	Tsp	Salt
1/2	Tsp	Baking powder
1/2	Tsp	Sugar
1/2	Cup	Raisins
1/2	Tsp	Powdered milk

DIRECTIONS

Mix the above ingredients with water into a dough and knead slightly. Follow instructions on page 4. Cook for 20-30 minutes. Turn over and brown the other side.

VARIATION

Add 1/2 cup mixed peel or cherries to the above mixture instead of raisins.

Skillet Bread

INGREDIENTS

1/2	Cup +	flour
4	Tsps	Baking powder
2	Tsps	Sugar
1/2	Tsp	Salt
2	Tbls	Shortening
1		Egg
		Water as needed

DIRECTIONS

Combine the dry ingredients in a bowl and cut into it the shortening. Add a beaten egg and enough water to make a soft dough.

Oil the skillet and heat until very hot. Shape the dough into a large round and put into the hot skillet. Put on a lid, turn the heat down, and cook for 15 minutes. Turn over and cook for an additional 10 minutes or until brown. Remove from the skillet to a plate to cool. Cut into wedges and serve.

Skillet Cornbread

INGREDIENTS

1	Cup	Yellow cornmeal
1 1/2	Tsp	Baking powder
1 1/2	Cups	Flour
3/4	Tsp	Salt
1	Tbl	Sugar
1/4	Cup	Melted butter
2		Eggs, well-beaten
1	Cup	Milk

DIRECTIONS

Put all the ingredients into a bowl and beat briskly until well blended.

Heat a heavy skillet and put in 1 tablespoon oil. Make sure the bottom of the skillet is well oiled. Pour in the batter and tip the skillet so the batter will cover the bottom evenly. Cook on one side for 10 minutes, then turn over and cook for another 10 minutes. Remove from the pan, cut into wedges, and serve hot with butter.

If the skillet does not heat evenly, use the asbestos pad under it.

Oatcakes
Cook little round cakes in the skillet

INGREDIENTS

1	Cup	Flour
2	Cups	Oatmeal
3	Tsps	Baking powder
1/2	Tsp	Baking soda
1	Tbl	Sugar
4	Tbls	Butter
1/2	Tsp	Salt
1		Egg (optional)
		Milk or water as needed

DIRECTIONS

Mix all the dry ingredients. Cut the butter into the mixture until it is well-blended. Add the egg to 1/2 cup milk and beat well. Add to the flour mixture and blend. Add more milk or water until you have a soft dough.

Turn onto a floured board and knead a few seconds. Pat the dough to 1/2-inch thickness and cut out little round cakes. Put into a slightly greased hot skillet, cover with lid, cook until brown on one side, and then turn over and cook on the other side. This takes about 15 minutes in all.

Drop Doughnuts

Spicy little doughnuts rolled in sugar

INGREDIENTS

1		Egg
1/3	Cup	Sugar
1 1/2	Cups	Flour
1/2	Cup	Milk
2	Tsps	Baking powder
		Pinch salt
1/8	Tsp	Nutmeg
2	Tbls	Shortening, melted

DIRECTIONS

Mix the above ingredients until the batter is smooth and thick. Heat 2-3 inches of oil in a saucepan until very hot. Drop the batter by teaspoons into the hot oil and cook until golden brown. Turn and cook the other side. When golden brown, remove from oil and drain on paper. Roll in plain or confectioners sugar.

Rice Doughnuts

These little doughnuts are from Fiji

INGREDIENTS

2	Cups	Sifted flour
4	Tsps	Baking powder
2	Tsps	Sugar
1	Cup	Cold cooked rice

DIRECTIONS

Mix the above ingredients together and add enough water to make a very thick batter. Heat 2-3 inches of oil in a saucepan, and when very hot, drop in the batter by teaspoons. Cook on one side; then turn over and cook until golden brown. Remove from the oil and drain on paper. Roll in confectioners sugar.

Pikelets Without Butter
A tasty kind of griddle cake

INGREDIENTS

1	Cup	Flour
2	Tsps	Cream of tartar
		Pinch salt
1		Egg
2	Tbls	Sugar
3/4	Cup	Milk
1	Tsp	Baking soda

DIRECTIONS

Sift the flour, salt, baking soda, and cream of tartar in a bowl. Add the sugar. Make a well in the center of the mixture. Break the egg and slowly add the milk, beating all the while. Pour a little batter on a hot greased skillet. When one side bubbles, turn it over and cook the other side. Repeat until all batter is used. Keep the pikelets covered with a towel to keep them warm and soft. Serve with butter and syrup.

VARIATION

Add 1/2 cup mixed peel, chopped dates, or raisins, or 1/2 teaspoon of cinnamon, cloves, or poppy or sesame seeds.

Banana Pikelets

Sprinkle with lemon juice and sugar

INGREDIENTS

2	Cups	Flour
2	Tsps	Baking powder
1/4	Tsp	Grated nutmeg
1	Tbl	Sugar
1 1/2	Cups	Milk
1	large	Egg (or two small)
2	Tbls	Melted butter
4		Bananas

DIRECTIONS

Sift flour, baking powder, and nutmeg. Add sugar. Combine beaten egg with milk and stir into the flour, making a smooth batter. Stir in the melted butter and thinly sliced bananas. Drop by spoonfuls into a hot greased skillet. Turn with spatula when top bubbles. Brown the other side. Stack and keep warm. Serve with butter and sprinkle with lemon juice and sugar.

VARIATIONS

1 cup of drained shredded pineapple may be used instead of bananas.

Easy Easy Gingerbread

Spiced with cinnamon, nutmeg, and ginger

INGREDIENTS

1/2	Cup	Boiling water
1/2	Cup	Butter or margarine
1	Cup	Molasses
2 1/2	Cups	Flour
1/2	Tsp	Salt
1/2	Tsp	Cinnamon
1	Tsp	Ginger
1/4	Tsp	Nutmeg
1 1/2	Tsp	Baking soda

(continued)

DIRECTIONS

Dissolve soda in 2 tablespoons of boiling water. Add the balance of boiling water to the butter and stir until butter has melted. Add molasses and stir well. Add the spices and salt while stirring. Add the flour and beat until the batter is smooth. Pour the dissolved baking soda over the batter and beat until it is well mixed into the batter.

Pour the batter into a well-oiled, hot saucepan that has been heated according to instructions for baking cakes on page 16. Cook over medium heat for 25-30 minutes. Check to see if cake is cooked; if not, lower heat and bake until done. Sometimes, depending on the flame, it takes up to 40 minutes. Turn out onto rack to cool. Serve plain or with whipped cream or topping.

CAKES AND ICINGS
Instructions for Baking Cakes

1. Cut a circle of white or brown paper the size of the bottom of the saucepan and set aside.

2. Light the stove and put asbestos pad on top of the flame.

3. Put 3/4 - 1 tablespoon oil in the bottom of saucepan.

4. Put lid on saucepan and set on asbestos pad. When lid is too hot to touch, turn flame down—a little lower than medium—so the oil won't smoke.

5. Make cake batter while saucepan is heating.

6. Take a pastry brush or small piece of tissue on a fork and spread the oil 3/4 of the way up the sides and over the bottom of saucepan.

7. Carefully put the circle of paper on the bottom of pan and oil, put on lid, and reheat for a few minutes.

8. Remove lid and quickly pour the cake batter into the saucepan. Spread batter towards the sides and leave a slight indentation in the middle. Put the lid on and cook for the required recipe time without removing the lid.

9. Test for doneness by inserting a toothpick or straw. If it is clean when removed, the cake is cooked.

10. Run a knife around the sides of the cake—especially if it's a sponge.

11. Set saucepan aside and let the cake cool for 5 minutes.

12. Turn the cake out onto a rack to cool.

13. Frost when cold. See page 29 for a basic creamy icing recipe.

IMPORTANT

Cake shouldn't stick if oil and heat are right.

Cake should be cooked in recommended time if the heat is right.

Quick White Cake

INGREDIENTS

1/2	Cup	Margarine
1	Cup	Sugar
2		Eggs
1/2	Cup	plus 2 1/2 Tsps Milk
1 1/2	Cups	Plain flour
2	Tbls	Cornstarch
1/2	Tsp	Salt
1 1/2	Tsps	Baking powder
1	Tsp	Vanilla

DIRECTIONS

Cream butter and sugar together until smooth. Add eggs, one at a time, and beat well. Sift the flour, cornstarch, salt and baking powder together. Add to the first mixture alternately with the milk. Beat well until smooth. Add vanilla.

Check the instructions on page 16 and cook for 30 minutes on a medium flame.

White Cake

White cake with just one egg

INGREDIENTS

3/4	Cup	Sugar
1/4	Cup	Shortening
1		Egg
1	Tsp	Vanilla
1 1/2	Cups	Flour
2	Tsps	Baking powder
1	Cup	Milk

DIRECTIONS

Cream together sugar, eggs, and shortening. Add milk and vanilla. Fold sifted dry ingredients into the milk mixture and stir to make a medium-thick batter.

Follow cooking instructions on page 16. Cook on medium flame for 30 minutes.

Banana Cake
Very light and delicious

INGREDIENTS

1	Cup	Flour
1/2	Tsp	Baking powder
1	Tsp	Baking soda
3/4	Cup	Slight milk
1/2	Cup	Butter
2		Eggs
1/2	Cup	Sugar
3-4		Bananas (according to size)

DIRECTIONS

Cream sugar and butter and add well-beaten eggs. Add sifted flour. Mash bananas well and add to the mixture. Dissolve baking soda in the milk and add to the batter. Beat well until batter is smooth. Pour the batter into a prepared oiled saucepan. Follow instructions on page 16. Bake for 30 minutes or until cake is done. Frost with banana icing made by mashing either banana essence or a banana into confectioners sugar.

Cherry and Sweet Orange Cake
Simple with instant pudding powder

INGREDIENTS

1	Packet	Orange instant pudding powder
1/2	Cup	Butter
1/2	Cup	Sugar
1		Egg
1 1/2	Cups	Flour
2	Tsps	Baking powder

DIRECTIONS

Mix 4 tablespoons of instant pudding powder in milk and leave to set. Cream the butter and sugar, then slowly beat in the set pudding and well-beaten egg. Add sifted flour and baking powder. Follow instructions on page 16 and cook for 30-40 minutes. When cold, split cake in half, fill with sweet orange filling, and frost. *(continued)*

FILLING

Mix 2 tablespoons of pudding powder in 1/2 cup milk; let set. Cream 4 tablespoons of butter and 1/4 cup sugar and add set pudding. Beat until fluffy. Add 2 tablespoons chopped cherries and spread between cake layers.

ICING

Beat 2 teaspoons pudding powder into 1/4 cup milk. When set, add 1 teaspoon butter and 2 cups confectioners sugar. Ice cake and top with cherries.

Easy Sponge Cake
Golden yellow, light, and fluffy

INGREDIENTS

3		Eggs, separated
1	Cup	Sugar
1	Cup	Flour
1	Tbl	Cornstarch
1	Tsp	Baking powder
1/4	Cup	Boiling water
1	Tsp	Butter, heaping
1	Tsp	Vanilla

DIRECTIONS

Beat three egg whites until stiff. Add sugar gradually and beat vigorously. Drop 3 unbeaten egg yolks into the whites and beat well. Sift and mix cornstarch, baking powder, and flour together and fold into the egg mixture. Add butter and vanilla to the boiling water. When butter is melted, add to the batter and gently fold in mix.

Follow baking instructions on page 16. Bake for 30 minutes over medium heat. Turn upside down onto rack, after running a knife around the edges. Ice with white frosting when cold.

20

Ginger Sponge
A spicy flavored sponge with 1 egg

INGREDIENTS

4	Tbls	Sugar
4	Tbls	Butter
1	Cup	+4 Tbls Flour
1	Tsp	Baking powder
1/2	Cup	+2 Tbls Milk
1		Egg
		Pinch salt
1/3	Tsp	Ground ginger
1/2	Tsp	Ground cinnamon
1/2	Tsp	Ground all spice

DIRECTIONS

Cream the butter and sugar. Separate the egg and add the well-beaten egg yolk. Sift the flour and baking powder, and add the spices and salt. Add to the egg mixture alternately with the milk. Beat the egg white until stiff, then fold into the batter.

Follow instructions on page 16 and bake for 30-40 minutes. Ice when cold or, after you have turned the cake onto a rack, turn it again onto a platter, light side up. Spread, while hot, with brown sugar and cinnamon mixed. Let cool and serve.

Eggless Fruit Cake
A rich cake that tastes better with age

INGREDIENTS

1	Cup	Sugar
2	Cups	Mixed fruit (raisins, currents, mixed peel, dates)
1	Cup	Cold water
1/2	Cup	Butter
1	Tsp	Vanilla
1	Tsp	Baking soda
2	Cups	Flour

(continued)

DIRECTIONS

Put the sugar, mixed fruit, butter, water, and vanilla into a saucepan and slowly bring to a boil. Boil gently for 3 minutes and then set aside to cool.

Mix well the baking soda and flour. Add the cooled fruit mixture and stir well. Pour into a hot, oiled saucepan and cook over asbestos pad on medium heat for 1 hour. When cold, store in an airtight container for a few days before eating.

Netta's 5 Cup Fruit Cake
A sailboat recipe from the Mediterranean

INGREDIENTS

1	Cup	Butter or margarine
1	Cup	Water
1	Cup	Fruit (dates, raisins, mixed peel)
1	Cup	Sugar
1	Cup	Self-raising cake flour
1	Tsp	Baking powder

DIRECTIONS

Heat butter and water in a saucepan until butter is melted. Add the fruit and sugar and mix well. Then add flour and baking powder. Mix well. Follow directions on page 16 and cook for 40-50 minutes on medium low heat. Test with a toothpick or straw after 40 minutes and adjust the flame accordingly.

Orange Cake
A delicate orange flavor

INGREDIENTS

3	Scant Tbls Butter	
1	Cup	Minus 2 Tbls Sugar
3		Eggs
		Pinch of salt
1 1/4	Cups	Flour
5	Tbls	Cornstarch
1	Tsp	Baking powder
		Rind and juice of 1 orange

DIRECTIONS

Cream the butter and sugar and add well-beaten eggs, pinch salt, and rind and juice of one orange. Sift the flour and cornstarch together with baking powder. Add to the sugar mixture and beat until smooth batter. Pour into a prepared oiled, hot saucepan that has been heated according to instructions on page 16. Bake for 30 minutes or until cake is done. Ice when cold with orange flavored frosting.

Orange Rum Cake
Orange-rum sauce is poured over the cake

INGREDIENTS

1	Cup	Butter or margarine
2	Cups	Sugar
		Rinds and juice from 2 large oranges
2		Eggs
2 1/2	Cups	Flour
2	Tsp	Baking powder
1	Tsp	Baking soda
1/2	Tsp	Salt
1	Cup	Buttermilk or sour milk
1	Cup	Chopped walnuts
		Rind and the juice from 1 lemon
2	Tbls	Rum

(continued)

DIRECTIONS

Cream the butter and 1 cup sugar until smooth. Add the orange and
lemon rinds and the eggs, one at a time. Add sifted dry ingredients alternately with buttermilk. Beat after each addition. Fold in the walnuts and
pour into an oiled hot saucepan. Follow instructions on page 16. Bake on
medium to low heat for approximately one hour. Test cake after 30
minutes.

To make the syrup, combine the fruit juices and strain into a saucepan.
Add remaining cup of sugar and rum. Heat just to the boiling point until
sugar has dissolved. Pour slowly over the cake while hot. Slice into
wedges and put into dessert dishes. Eat with a fork.

Marble Cake
Pink and brown marble effect

INGREDIENTS

1/2	Cup	Butter
3/4	Cup	Sugar
2		Eggs
2	Cups	Flour
1	Tsp	Baking powder
		Pinch of salt
1/2	Cup	Milk
1	Tsp	Vanilla
		Few drops red food coloring
1	Tbl	Cocoa
2	Tsps	Boiling water
2	Tsps	Sugar

DIRECTIONS

Cream butter and sugar until light and fluffy. Add one egg at a time, beating well after each addition. Sift flour, baking powder, and salt. Add them
to the cream mixture alternately with the milk and stir in gradually. Put
1/2 the mixture into a second bowl and stir in vanilla and food coloring.
Mix the cocoa, sugar, and boiling water into a smooth paste and mix into
the other half of batter. Prepare the saucepan according to instructions on
page 16. Pour the batter from one bowl onto the top of the other. **Do not
mix.** Pour them both into the saucepan, scraping with a spatula from the
bottom of the bowl in strokes. This will marble the batter. Bake for 30
minutes or until cake is cooked. Frost when cold with chocolate icing.

Date Cake From Sudan
Just one egg to this easy cake

INGREDIENTS

1	Cup	Sugar
1/4	Cup	Margarine or butter
1		Egg
1 1/2	Cups	Flour
1/2	Tsp	Salt
1	Tsp	Baking soda
		Slightly less than one cup milk
1	Tsp	Vanilla
1/2	Cup	Chopped dates
2	Tbls	Water

DIRECTIONS

Cream the sugar and butter until light. Add the egg and half the milk. Sift flour and salt and add alternately with the rest of the milk. Use just enough milk to make a medium batter. Mix the baking soda with the water and add to the batter. Beat until smooth. Fold in the dates.

Follow the instructions on page 16 and cook for 45 minutes on medium heat. Ice when cold.

Sultan's Loaf
Spicy flavored cake

INGREDIENTS

1	Tbl	Corn syrup
1	Cup	Water
1	Cup	Sugar
1/2	Cup	Raisins
1/2	Cup	Butter
2	Cups	Flour
1	Tsp	Baking powder
1/2	Tsp	Cinnamon
1	Tsp	Ginger
1/2	Tsp	All spice
1/2	Tsp	Baking soda

DIRECTIONS

Put syrup, water, sugar, raisins, and butter into a saucepan, stir, and bring almost to a boil. Add baking soda. Remove from flame and set aside to cool. Sift the flour and combine the dry ingredients. When the raisin mixture is cool, pour it over the dry ingredients and mix thoroughly.

Pour into a saucepan prepared according to instructions on page 13 and bake over medium-low heat for approximately 1 hour. Cool on rack. Cake will keep for weeks in an airtight container.

Peanut Butter Cake
Ice with chocolate frosting

INGREDIENTS

1/2	Cup	Smooth peanut butter
1/4	Cup	Butter
1 1/2	Cups	Brown sugar
2		Eggs
2	Cups	Flour
2	Tsps	Baking powder
1/2	Tsp	Baking soda
1	Tsp	Salt
1	Cup	Milk
1	Tsp	Vanilla

DIRECTIONS

Cream the peanut butter with butter. Add brown sugar and beat until light and fluffy. Add the eggs, one at a time, and beat well. Sift the dry ingredients together. Add the vanilla to the milk. Add these alternately to the peanut mixture until all the ingredients have been combined.

Follow instructions on page 16. Cook on medium heat for 30 minutes.

Wacky, Wacky Chocolate Cake
Moist open textured cake without eggs

INGREDIENTS

1 1/2	Cups	Plain Flour
1	Cup	Sugar
4	Tbls	Cocoa
1	Tsp	Baking soda
1/2	Tsp	Salt
5	Tbls	Butter or margarine
1	Tbl	Vinegar
1	Tsp	Vanilla
1	Cup	Boiling water

(continued)

DIRECTIONS

Sift flour and mix with other dry ingredients in a bowl. In another bowl combine the rest of the ingredients and heat in a saucepan. When the butter mixture has melted, add it all at once to the dry mixture. Stir until blended, but do not beat, to make a medium batter.

Follow directions given on page 16. Cook for 30 minutes on medium flame. When cold, ice with chocolate frosting.

Uncooked Chocolate Cake
Just mix, press into pan, and frost

INGREDIENTS

1/2	Cup	Butter
1		Egg
2	Tbls	Cocoa
1	Tsp	Vanilla
1/2	Cup	Sugar
3/4	Cup	Chopped walnuts
1	Cup	Graham crackers, crumbled

DIRECTIONS

Melt the butter in a saucepan. Add sugar, cocoa, and beaten egg. Stir and bring to a boil. Simmer for 1 minute, then add the remaining ingredients. Press into a well-greased cake pan and set aside. Make chocolate icing and spread on the cake. Let set for an hour; then cut into squares.

Honeysuckle Cake
Uncooked cake with condensed milk

INGREDIENTS

1/2	Can	Condensed sweet milk
3/4	Cup	Rolled oats or coconut
1/2	Cup	Chopped walnuts
25		Crushed dry cookies or graham crackers
1 3/4	Cups	Cake crumbs
		Pinch of salt
		Grated rind of 1 orange
1/2	Cup	Melted butter

DIRECTIONS

Combine all ingredients in order given. Press into greased square cake pan. Set aside and make the following icing.

ICING

2	Tbls	Melted butter
4	Tsps	Orange juice
3/4	Cup	Confectioners sugar
2	Tbls	Condensed Milk

DIRECTIONS

Mix the above ingredients together and spread on cake. Allow to set; then cut into squares.

Unbaked Fruitcake

INGREDIENTS

1 Lb.	(2 Cups)	Sweet Cracker crumbs
1 Lb.	(2 Cups)	Raisins
1 Lb.	(2 Cups)	Marshmallows
3/4	Cup	Milk, or halved with rum or brandy
2	Cups	Candied fruit, dates, cherries, raisins
4	Cups	Whole walnuts

DIRECTIONS

Crush the crackers into crumbs, combine the raisins, fruit, cherries, and nuts. Scald the milk in a double boiler, add the marshmallows, and melt over boiling water. Pour over the fruit-crumb mixture and mix with hands.

Line two loaf pans with foil and pour in the crumb mixture. Press the mixture into the loaf pans until even on top. Decorate with whole nuts. Chill for several hours. Makes 6 pounds of cake.

Attention: You can use any sweet cookie, graham crackers, or wafers or add a few crushed ginger snaps for a different flavor.

Basic Creamy Icing
Add your choice of flavoring and coloring

INGREDIENTS

6	Tbls	Softened butter
3	Tbls	Powdered milk
3 1/2	Cups	Confectioners sugar
3	Tbls	Hot water

DIRECTIONS

Place the butter in a bowl, add powdered milk, and blend. Add choice of flavoring and the confectioners sugar. Mix to a spreading consistency with hot water.

VARIATIONS

Add 2 Tsps instant coffee.

Add 2 Tsps cocoa, more if you want darker icing.

Add 1 Tsp instant coffee and 1 Tsp cocoa.

Add small amount ground ginger to the water.

Add just enough coloring to get the desired color. Be sure to mix well after each drop of coloring.

Add 1/2 Tsp essence to icing just before adding the water. Be careful to use less for the strong flavors.

PIES AND FILLINGS

What moistens the lips,
What brightens the eye,
What calls back the past,
Like rich pumkin pie?
—Old jingle

Instructions for Making Pies in a Skillet

You will need:
   7-inches non-stick skillet
   5 x 5 x 1/4 inch asbestos pad with 6 small holes drilled in it
   Piece of aluminum foil. Fold it to make a lid for the skillet.
      It should not fit tightly as steam must escape.

To cook pies:
1. Always put the asbestos pad on the flame before you start making the crust. Use a high flame. The asbestos must be very hot, and the pie shell must be cooked on high heat.

2. After the pie dough is made, form it into a ball, but do not knead.

3. Roll out the crust on a slightly floured board. Make it into a circle that will fit the bottom and sides of the skillet.

4. Place the rolled dough in the skillet. The dough should come just to the top of the pan.

5. Prick the bottom and sides of the dough with a fork.

6. Place the foil lid on top of the skillet and cook for 15 minutes on the very hot asbestos pad, which is over a high flame.

7. When cooked, remove crust from skillet and put on a plate to cool.

Important
If you are making more than one crust, be sure to let the skillet cool completely before putting the next crust in. If you don't, the crust will not hold its shape.

Single Pie Crust

INGREDIENTS

1/2	Cup	Flour
3	Tbls	Shortening
1/2	Tsp	Sugar
		Dash of salt
		Water

DIRECTIONS

Sift the flour into a bowl and add salt and sugar. Use a fork to cut the shortening into the flour—mashing style. Add just enough water, approximately 1/8 cup, to make a stiff dough.

Follow the instructions on page 31.

Double Pie Crust

Double the amounts used for a single pie crust and follow the same directions. Use a little more than half the dough for the bottom crust. When that has cooked, let the skillet cool until you can touch it with your hands. Roll out the remaining dough to fit the bottom of the skillet only. Prick it thoroughly with a fork. Put on foil lid and cook as before.

Fill the bottom pie shell with a cooled cooked filling and put the second crust on top of it. Sprinkle with a little confectioners sugar if you like.

VARIATIONS

Cook narrow strips of dough in the bottom of the skillet for a top open crust. Fill the pie crust with a cooked berry filling and lay the cooked strips of pastry across the top.

Follow the recipe for single crust pastry and add 2 Tbls of desiccated coconut.

Add 1 1/2 Tbls of sesame seeds to the pastry dough.

Add 4 Tbls of cheese to the pastry dough. Put an extra piece of aluminum foil on top of the asbestos pad when cooking as cheese burns easily. Delicious for apple pies and savory tart shells.

Cinnamon Pastry
Lemon and cinnamon flavor

INGREDIENTS

1/2	Cup	Flour
3	Level Tbls	Shortening
		Juice from 1/2 lemon
		Dash salt
1/4	Tsp	Cinnamon
		Sprinkling of sugar

DIRECTIONS

Mix the flour, salt, and cinnamon together. Cut in the shortening with a fork—mashing style. Sprinkle 1/4 teaspoon sugar over the flour mixture and stir once. Add the lemon juice to enough cold water to make approximately 1/8 cup. Add to the flour mixture, stirring to make a stiff dough. Roll out on a slightly floured board and follow instructions given on page 31.

Cornflakes or Bread Crumbs Pie Shell

INGREDIENTS

3/4	Cup	Brown sugar
3	Tbls	Honey
1	scant Tbl	Butter
2	Tbls	Orange juice
3	Cups	Cornflakes or 2 1/2 Cups fine bread crumbs

DIRECTIONS

Stir brown sugar, honey, butter, and orange juice over low flames until sugar dissolves. Boil rapidly until a little of the mixture dropped into cold water forms a soft ball. Pour mixture over cornflakes or fine bread crumbs. Mix lightly. Press mixture around the sides and bottom of a greased 9-inch pie plate. Set aside to cool and set while making the filling.

Fill with chocolate, vanilla, caramel, or any creamed pie filling.

Crumb Pie Shell

Easy, no cooking pie shell

INGREDIENTS

2	Tbls	Sugar
3	Tbls	Butter
1 1/2	Cups	Cookie crumbs or graham crackers

DIRECTIONS

Melt the butter in a saucepan and add sugar. Cook on low flame until the sugar has dissolved. Mix in the crumbs until evenly blended. Press into a pie dish. Cool and fill with any type of filling.

(continued)

VARIATIONS

Add 2 tablespoons cocoa to cookie crumbs.

Add 2 tablespoons coconut flakes to the crumbs.

Add 1/2 teaspoon cinnamon to the crumbs.

Use brown sugar instead of white sugar.

Basic Cream Pie Filling

INGREDIENTS

1 1/2	Cup	Water
1/4	Cup	Flour
4	Tbls	Milk powder
1/4	Tsp	Salt
1	Tbl	Butter
1/2	Tsp	Vanilla

DIRECTIONS

Put 1 cup water in a saucepan and bring to boil. Mix flour, milk powder, sugar, and salt in the remaining 1/2 cup of water and slowly add, stirring constantly, to the boiling water. Cook until mixture is thick. Remove from heat and add butter and vanilla. Fill cooled pie shell with any fruit and pour the cream filling over the top. Set aside to cool and set.

Butterscotch Pie Filling

INGREDIENTS

1	Cup	Brown sugar
2	Tsps	Butter (heaping)
2	Tbls	Flour
2		Eggs
1	Cup	Milk

DIRECTIONS

Cream butter, sugar, and flour together. Mix well-beaten eggs into the milk and heat in a saucepan until just boiling. Remove from the flame and pour over the first mixture, stirring to keep smooth. Pour all back into the saucepan and cook until the mixture is thick. Cool slightly, then pour into a cooked pie shell.

Pumpkin Pie Filling

Pumpkin, pudding mix, and spices

INGREDIENTS

1	Package	Vanilla pudding powder
1 1/2	Cups	Canned pumpkin
1/4	Tsp	Ground ginger
1/4	Tsp	Ground cinnamon
	Dash	Ground cloves
	Dash	Nutmeg

DIRECTIONS

Make the pudding according to the directions on the package. Add the spices. When cooked, add the pumpkin, return to the heat, and just boil. Remove from stove and let cool. Pour into a cooked pie shell. Let set and serve with whipped cream. Make enough filling for two 6-7-inch pie shells.

Apple Pie Filling

INGREDIENTS

		Apples
		Apples
1/2	Cup	Sugar
1/8	Tsp	Cinnamon
1	Tbl	Butter
		Corn starch
		Water

DIRECTIONS

Peel and core enough apples to fill a pie shell. Put in saucepan and add sugar, cinnamon, and butter plus enough water to keep the apples from sticking to the bottom of the pan while cooking. After apples are soft, add enough corn starch mixed with water to thicken the juice. Pour into pastry shell when cool. Put the top pastry shell in place. Sprinkle with confectioners sugar and set aside to cool.

VARIATIONS

Add 1/2 to 1 cup of blackberries and omit the cinnamon.

Use strips of pastry to cover the filling instead of a complete top.

Apple and Date Filling

INGREDIENTS

4		Apples, cored, peeled, and sliced
1	Cup	Dates, pitted and cut in half
1	Piece	Preserved ginger, chopped finely, or
1/2	Tsp	Ground ginger
1/2	Cup	Water
1/4	Cup	Sugar or enough to sweeten
1/2	Tsp	Cinnamon
		Juice from 1/2 Lemon and grated rind

DIRECTIONS

Simmer the above ingredients together except the lemon juice. When apples are tender, let mixture cool. Stir in the lemon juice and spoon the filling into a cooked pie shell.

Lemon Pie Filling

INGREDIENTS

1 1/2	Cups	Water
1/4	Cup	Sugar
		Grated rind from 1 lemon
		Juice from 2 lemons to make up to 1/4 Cup
		Dab of butter
1/4	Cup	Cornstarch
1		Egg

DIRECTIONS

Put 1 cup of water in saucepan with sugar and lemon rinds. Boil until sugar dissolves. Mix the corn starch in the remaining water and slowly add to the boiling mixture. Stir constantly and cook until very thick. Add the butter and remove from the heat. Beat the egg slightly and slowly add to the mixture, stirring constantly so egg doesn't cook. Beat until smooth, then add the lemon juice. Mix well and let set until lukewarm. Pour into a cooked pie shell.

Poach meringues and place on top of filling (see recipe on page 41).

Lime or Lemon Pie Filling

A very sweet filling

INGREDIENTS

1	can	Sweetened condensed milk
		Juice from 3-6 limes or lemons

DIRECTIONS

Pour the condensed milk into a bowl and add the juice from the limes or lemons, one at a time. Beat well with each addition. A small amount of juice sets the milk, but use the rest according to your taste.

(continued)

VARIATIONS

You can also use this recipe as a topping for apples, apricots, or peaches.
Slice the fruit and put a layer into a cooked pie shell and top with filling.
Pureed fruit can also be used as a base for this pie filling.

Fruit Pie Filling
Orange and banana filling

INGREDIENTS

2	Cups	Milk
2		Eggs, separated
3	Tbls	Cornstarch
1/2	Cup	Sugar
4		Oranges
1		Banana

DIRECTIONS

Mix the sugar and cornstarch with a little milk. Heat the rest of the milk in a
saucepan and slowly add the cornstarch mixture. Stir and cook, until thick,
over low flame. Remove from the heat and add well-beaten egg yolks. Return
to heat and cook a few minutes longer.

Peel and slice the oranges very thin. Remove pits and any extra pits.
Mash the banana until smooth and add to the mixture together with the
sliced oranges. Cook slowly and fold in stiffly beaten egg whites. Remove
from stove and pour into a pastry shell.

Pineapple Pie Filling

INGREDIENTS

1	Can	Crushed pineapple
		Add enough water to make 1 3/4 Cups
1/4	Cup	Cornstarch
1		Egg
		Dab butter
		Enough sugar to sweeten
		Dash salt

DIRECTIONS

Put the pineapple, salt, and sugar into a saucepan. Heat until it just boils. Mix the cornstarch with a little water to make a paste and slowly pour it into the hot mixture, stirring to prevent lumps. Cook until thickened. Remove from the stove, add the butter, and slowly add a well-beaten egg. Let cool; then pour into a cooked pie shell.

Chocolate Pie Filling

INGREDIENTS

1 3/4	Cups	Milk
1/4	Cup	Sugar (plus 2 Tbls)
3	Tsps	Corn starch (heaping)
3	Tsps	Cocoa (heaping)
	Small	Dab butter
		Dash salt

DIRECTIONS

Put 1 1/2 cups of milk into a saucepan, add sugar, and bring just to a boil. Mix the corn starch and cocoa into the remaining ¼ cup of milk. Slowly, stirring constantly, add the corn starch mixture to the boiling milk. Add butter and salt and heat until thickened. Cook for 2 minutes more. When lukewarm, pour into cooked pastry shell.

(continued)

VARIATIONS

Top the shredded coconut. Add 1 tablespoon sesame seeds to the filling before pouring into the pie shell.

Poached Meringues
Use to top pies or custards

INGREDIENTS

2		Eggs
		Pinch of salt
1/4	Cup	Sugar
3	Cups	Milk

DIRECTIONS

Beat together egg whites until they have soft peaks. Add salt and beat a little longer. Add sugar and beat until there are stiff peaks.

In a skillet heat milk to a simmer. Drop the meringue into the milk by teaspoons. Cook slowly uncovered for about 5 minutes until set. Lift out and set on a plate to cool.

Make custard out of the egg yolks and milk.

You can top the custard with the meringues or pour berries or fruit into a serving dish and top with custard and then with the meringues.

42

COOKIES

*Sugar and spice
and all things nice.*
  —Robert Southey

Instructions for Making Cookies
Baked Cookies:

1. Put asbestos pad on top of high flame.

2. Put a large iron skillet, with lid on, on top of asbestos pad.

3. Test heat by dropping a drop of water onto skillet. When it barely sizzles, the pan is hot enough.

4. Turn down the flame and keep temperature even.

5. Slightly oil the skillet when hot.

6. Now you are ready to bake the cookies. Follow directions in the recipes.

7. When spooning batter onto the hot skillet, avoid the center of the frying pan. Place around the edges instead.

8. Place a lid over the skillet while cookies are baking.

9. It takes 15-20 minutes to cook most cookies, and they should be golden brown on both sides. Adjust the flame accordingly.

Boiled Cookies:

These cookies are made with a fudge-like mixture that binds together various fruits, nutmeats, and the like to make delicious drop cookies.

Brandy Snaps and Curls:

Follow the instructions in the recipes on pages 49 and 50.

Chocolate Chip Cookies
Use 1 bar of sweet dark chocolate

INGREDIENTS

2	Tbls	Shortening
1/4	Cup	Sugar (plus 1 Tbl)
1	Cup	Flour
1	Tsp	Baking powder
1		Egg
1/4	Tsp	Vanilla
1	Bar	Dark Chocolate

DIRECTIONS

Mix and cream shortening, egg, and sugar until smooth. Add the dry ingredients and beat until batter is smooth. Break the chocolate bar into small pieces and add to the batter.

Drop 1/2 teaspoonfuls onto a slightly oiled, hot skillet, according to instructions on page 42. Make sure there is room for the cookies to spread. Put lid on skillet and bake for 10 minutes. Gently turn the cookies over and bake uncovered for another 5 minutes. Cool on rack. Repeat with the rest of the batter.

Makes approximately 12 cookies. If doubling the recipe, do not add another egg.

VARIATION

Use 1 cup of shredded coconut instead of the chocolate.

Peanut Butter Cookies
A syrupy, nutty flavor

INGREDIENTS

2	Tbls	Margarine
1/4	Cup	Sugar
1	Tbl	Corn syrup
1 1/2	Tbls	Milk
1 1/2	Tbls	Peanut butter
1	Cup	Flour
1	Tsp	Baking powder
	Dash	Salt

DIRECTIONS

Cream together sugar, margarine, milk, peanut butter, and syrup. Add the dry ingredients. Mix well and then knead until mixture leaves the side of the bowl. Roll into small balls. Press with a fork to flatten.

Cook around the outside of a prepared skillet. See instructions on page 42. Cook for 15 minutes with lid on. Gently turn cookies over and cook with lid on for another 5 minutes. Remove from skillet and cool on rack.

Skillet Fried Cookies
Condensed milk, nuts, coconuts, chocolate

INGREDIENTS

1/2	Cup	Butter
1	Cup	Chopped nuts
7	Tbls	Coconut
3/4	Cup	Chocolate chips
1 1/2	Cups	Graham cracker or dry cookie crumbs
2	Cups	Condensed sweet milk (Scant)

(continued)

DIRECTIONS

Melt the butter in a heavy skillet and remove from the heat. Add the remaining ingredients in layers—nuts, coconuts, crumbs, and chocolate. Slowly pour condensed milk over the top. Cover with lid or foil.

Put skillet on top of asbestos pad and cook over medium heat for approximately 25 minutes. Test the mixture with a toothpick for doneness. When toothpick comes out clean when inserted in the middle, the cookies are done. Remove from the heat and uncover. Set aside to cool. When cool, cut into slices, remove from skillet, and set on a rack to finish cooling. Store in airtight containers.

Nutty Joys
Dates and cinnamon flavor

INGREDIENTS

6	Tbls	Margarine
1/2	Cup	Chopped dates
1/2	Cup	Sugar
1/2	Tsp	Baking soda
1	Cup	Flour
1		Egg
1	Tsp	Cinnamon
Scant	Tbl	Water

DIRECTIONS

Beat the egg and sugar and add the melted butter. Add the rest of the ingredients, except the soda and water. Mix well and add the soda and water mixture last. If batter is too stiff, add a little milk.

Drop small spoonfuls into a prepared skillet. See instructions on page 42. Bake on low heat, with lid on, for 15 minutes. Gently turn cookies over and cook for another 5 minutes. Cool on rack.

Boiled Cookies

Nuts, oatmeal, and coconut

INGREDIENTS

1	Cup	Sugar
1/4	Cup	(plus 2 Tbls) Milk
1	Tsp	Vanilla
1/3	Cup	Chopped nuts
1/4	Cup	Butter
1 1/2	Cups	Quick cooking oats
1/3	Cup	Shredded coconut

DIRECTIONS

Mix oats, coconut, and chopped nuts together. Heat the sugar, butter, and milk in a heavy saucepan until they boil. Boil for 3 minutes. Remove from the heat and quickly add the vanilla and dry ingredients. Stir until thoroughly mixed. Drop by teaspoon onto waxed paper or an oiled tray and dry for several hours before storing in an airtight container.

Judy Cookies

Little round balls rolled in confectioners sugar or coconut

INGREDIENTS

4	Tsps	Cocoa
3/4	Cup	Cold water
1	Cup	White sugar
2	Cup	Graham cracker crumbs or equivalent
1	Tsp	Vanilla
1/2	Cup	Chopped nuts

DIRECTIONS

Mix and boil for 5 minutes the cocoa, water, and sugar. Then mix in the cracker crumbs, vanilla, and nuts. When the mixture is cool enough to handle, shape it into small balls and roll in confectioners sugar or coconut. Set aside to cool. Very easy to make.

Easy Unbaked Chocolate Cookies
Chocolate goodies from the ketch Tzu Hang

INGREDIENTS

3	Tbls	Butter
2	Cups	Sugar
1/2	Cup	Milk
6	Tbls	Cocoa
1	Tsp	Vanilla
3	Cup	Quick cooking oatmeal

DIRECTIONS

Put butter, sugar, milk, and cocoa into a suacepan and cook until the mixture forms a soft ball when dropped in cold water—the way you test fudge. Remove from heat, add vanilla, and let sit until just starting to cool. Add the oatmeal and mix well until the oatmeal is completely coated. Spoon onto a well-greased cookie sheet or waxed paper the desired size cookie you want. Let cool. Serve at once or store in an airtight container.

VARIATIONS

Add 1 cup coconut mixed with oatmeal.

Add 2 tablespoons peanut butter before adding oatmeal.

Add 1 tablespoon rum instead of vanilla.

Add 1/2 cup walnuts or peanuts before adding oatmeal.

Add 1/2 cup raisins before adding oatmeal.

Cocoa-Peanut Butter Unbaked Cookies
A fudgy, peanut tasting cookie

INGREDIENTS

3 1/2	Cups	Oatmeal
2	Tbls	Peanut Butter
4	Tbls	Shredded coconut
1	Tsp	Vanilla
1/2	Cup	Milk
2	Cups	Sugar
3	Tbls	Butter
3	Tbls	Cocoa

DIRECTIONS

Mix the oatmeal and coconut and set aside. Mix milk, sugar, butter, cocoa, and peanut butter in a saucepan. Boil until the soft ball stage when tested in cold water. Add vanilla, oatmeal, and coconut. Drop spoonfuls onto wax paper or oiled foil and allow to stand for 15 minutes or until cold and set.

Brandy Snaps

All you need is batter, three pieces of foil, and a skillet

INGREDIENTS

1/4	Cup	Butter
1/4	Cup	Corn syrup
1/3	Cup	Sugar (brown preferable)
1/3	Cup	Flour
3/4	Tsp	Ground ginger

DIRECTIONS

Heat syrup, butter, and sugar in a small saucepan, over asbestos pad. Stir until melted. Stir in the flour and ginger. Let cool.

Heat cast iron skillet on asbestos pad until its base is hot. Turn down flame. Tear off three pieces of foil, one for a lid and the others the size of the bottom of the skillet. Oil the second two pieces and drop a teaspoon of batter on each. Put one piece of foil on the hot skillet bottom and cover with foil lid loosely. Cook for 5 minutes. Snap should be bubbly and barely brown when cooked. Adjust heat accordingly. Remove the cooked snap and foil and replace it with the next one.

While warm, carefully roll the snap loosely onto a well-oiled wooden spoon handle. Be careful not to break the foil. Slide the snap off of handle onto a plate. Repeat the above procedures until all the batter is used. Makes 10-12. Fill with fresh whipped cream or mock cream (see recipes on page 71).

50

Caramel Curls

Caramel coconut curls to fill with cream

INGREDIENTS

1/4	Cup	Butter or margarine
1/2	Cup	Brown sugar, packed
1		Egg
1/2	Tsp	Vanilla
1/8	Tsp	Salt
3	Tbls	Flour
1/4	Cup	Coconut

DIRECTIONS

Cream the butter and sugar and add the egg and vanilla. Beat well and add salt, flour, and coconut. Beat until smooth.

Heat a cast iron skillet on the asbestos pad until its base is hot. Turn heat down. Tear off three pieces of foil approximately 8 inches wide. One is for a lid and two to cook curls on. Oil one piece of foil in the center and drop a heaping teaspoon of batter into the center and spread with spoon until the edges are barely brown but the top is still moist to touch. Remove from the pan and replace with the next spoon handle. Slide off handle onto plate to cool. Repeat the procedure until all the batter is used. Fill with whipped cream or mock cream when cold (See recipes on pages 71 and 72).

Other Desserts

CREPES AND SAUCES

Basic Crepes
Fill with fruit, vegetables, or seafood and cover with delicious sauces

INGREDIENTS

1/4	Cup	Sugar
1/4	Tsp	Cinnamon
1/2	Cup	Cream or evaporated milk
2		Eggs
1	Tsp	Salt
1	Cup	Water
1/4	Tsp	Vanilla
3/4	Cup	Flour

DIRECTIONS

Beat the egg well and slowly add salt, sugar, and cinnamon. Combine the water and cream and add alternately with flour.

Oil and heat the skillet. When hot, pour in 2 tablespoons of batter. Tip the skillet so the batter will spread evenly. When brown, turn over and brown the other side. Turn only once. When crepe is cooked, remove from skillet and stack on a warmed platter. When all the crepes are cooked, fill them with the desired filling. Roll up and place on a warmed platter. Spoon sauce, honey, or sugar over them, depending on the filling.

Banana Crepes

DIRECTIONS

Follow the basic recipe for crepes. When the crepes are cooked, spread each one with butter. Cut bananas in quarters lengthwise after they have been peeled. Put one quarter on a crepe and roll up. Set aside on warm platter. When all crepes are rolled, pour the following sauce over them and serve.

SAUCE

4	Tbls	Butter
1/2	Cup	Brown sugar
1/2	Tsp	Cinnamon
1/4	Tsp	Nutmeg
1/3	Cup	Red Wine

Heat butter in a saucepan, and when melted, add the other ingredients. When it is very hot, but not boiling, remove from stove and pour over the crepes.

Crepes and Berries

DIRECTIONS

Use the basic recipe for the crepes. When crepes are cooked, spread each one with butter and fill with any type of berry. Sprinkle with sugar and roll up. Set on warmed platter and make sauce.

SAUCE

1/4	Cup	Light corn syrup
2	Tbls	Lemon juice
1	Tbl	Cornstarch
1/2	Cup	Sugar
1/4	Cup	Water

DIRECTIONS

Mix the above ingredients in a saucepan and slowly heat over low flame. Stir constantly until the suace has thickened. Add extra berries to the sauce if desired. Pour over the warmed crepes and serve.

Mincemeat Crepes with Rum Sauce

Use the basic recipe to make the crepes. When they are cooked, spread each
one with butter, put 1 tablespoon mincemeat on one side, roll up, and set on
a warmed platter. Make the following sauce.

SAUCE

1/4	Cup	Butter
1/2	Cup	Sugar
1		Egg, beaten
1	Tsp	Grated lemon rind
1/2	Cup	Rum

DIRECTIONS

Melt the butter in a skillet and add sugar, rinds, and rum. Stir over low
heat until the sugar is melted. Add a few spoons of the rum mixture to a
beaten egg. Beat until fluffy and add the egg mixture to the rest of the
rum mixture. Mix well and dribble over the warmed crepes. Serve.

BARS, SQUARES, AND ICINGS

Instructions for Cooking Bars and Squares

1. Before starting to mix the ingredients for bars or squares, light the stove and put the asbestos pad on top of flame.

2. Put a heavy saucepan with a lid on the pad and heat until just warm. Remove saucepan and set aside while making the basic bar mixture. Do not take the asbestos pad off of the flame.

3. Slightly oil the bottom of the saucepan and press the bar mixture into it.

4. Put on the lid, set on the asbestos pad, and cook on medium-low heat for 20 minutes or the recommended recipe time.

5. Cut a circle approximately 7 inches in diameter that will fit into the saucepan from cardboard or stiff plastic, or use a plate.

6. Put the cardboard circle on top of the cooked bar. Turn the saucepan upside down, holding the cardboard over the bar, and ease the bar out of the saucepan.

7. Place a plate on top of the bar while in this position and turn the whole thing over again so the pale side of the bar will be upright.

Basic Bars

This recipe makes three bar bases. Add one of the following 8 recipes to each base for different flavors.

INGREDIENTS

1/2	Cup	Soft margarine
1	Cup	White sugar
1		Egg
2	Cups	Flour
1	Tsp	Baking powder
1/4	Tsp	Salt

DIRECTIONS

Cream the butter and add the sugar and egg. Beat until light and fluffy. Sift the flour, baking powder, and salt. Add to the butter mixture. Mix well and divide into three portions. Add one of the flavorings given on page 56 to each portion. Knead lightly on a floured board so the flavors will permeate the dough.

Pat the dough into a 7 inch circle and put into a warmed saucepan.

Follow the instructions for cooking bars on page 54. Ice while warm, then set aside to cool. Cut into bar shapes when cold.

Flavors and Icings for Basic Bars

Lemon Caraway Seed Bars

Add 1/2 tsp caraway seed and 1/2 tsp grated lemon rind.

ICING

Mix one cup of confectioners sugar and enough juice from the lemon to make a smooth paste. Ice while still warm.

Cinnamon Chocolate Bars

Add 1 Tbl cocoa and 1/2 tsp cinnamon.

Ice with chocolate frosting

Cinnamon Bars

Add 1/2 tsp cinnamon. Ice with chocolate frosting.

Orange Raisin Bars

Add grated rind from 1/2 orange and 1/4 cup raisins, chopped fine.

ICING

Mix 1 cup confectioners sugar and enough juice from the orange to make a smooth paste. Ice while still warm.

Orange Walnut Bars

Add 1 Tbl grated orange peel and 1/4 cup walnuts chopped very fine. Save a little of the nut meat to sprinkle on top of icing.

ICING

Mix 1 cup of confectioners sugar with enough juice from the orange to make a smooth paste. Ice while still warm.

Jam Bars

Spread strawberry or raspberry jam on top of cooked bar. Ice with vanilla icing when bar is cold.

Coconut Jam Bars

Spread the cooked bar with jam and sprinkle on coconut.

Date Bars

Boil 1/4 cup pitted dates with the juice from 1/2 a lemon in a saucepan with enough brown sugar to sweeten. Just cover the dates with water and boil until mixture thickens. Cool and spread over the bar base.

Ice with vanilla icing or sprinkle with a layer of coconut.

Coconut Bars
Coconut base with chocolate icing

INGREDIENTS

1	Cup	Flour
1/2	Cup	Sugar
1/2	Tsp	Vanilla
1	Cup	Coconut
1/2	Cup	Butter

DIRECTIONS

Put the flour, coconut, and sugar into a bowl. Melt the butter and add the vanilla and butter to the dry ingredients. Stir well until the mixture is crumbly. Follow the directions for cooking bars, on page 54. Make the following icing and spread on the bar while still warm.

ICING

1	Cup	Confectioners Sugar
1	Tbl	Cocoa
1	Tbl	Butter
		Water or milk

Mix confectioners sugar, cocoa, and butter together and add a little milk or water to make a smooth paste that will spread easily.

Chocolate Peppermint Squares
Uncooked, mouthwatering goodies

INGREDIENTS

1/2	Cup	Butter
3/4	Cup	Sugar
1	Tbl	Cocoa
1		Egg
1/2	Tsp	Peppermint essence
1	Cup	Crushed wafers or graham crackers

DIRECTIONS

Heat the butter, sugar, and cocoa in a saucepan until melted. Add the egg and beat well with a rotary beater. Cook a further minute, stirring all the time. Add the essence and crushed crackers. Mix well and turn into 8 x 12 pan. Press firmly and leave to set.

ICING

1 1/2	Cup	Confectioners sugar
1	Tbl	Vanilla custard powder
1	Tsp	Butter
		Few drops green coloring
		Few drops peppermint essence

DIRECTIONS

Blend the sugar and custard powder together and stir in melted butter. Add a flavoring and coloring to suit your taste and mix the icing to spreading consistency with a few drops of water if necessary. When base has set, ice thinly and leave overnight to set completely. Cut into about 48 dainty squares.

Chocolate Brownies

Three steps to the finished product

Oil a square cake pan and set aside.

Make chocolate icing:

ICING INGREDIENTS

1	Cup	Confectioners sugar
1	Tbl	Cocoa
1	Tbl	Margarine
		Enough water to make spreading easy

DIRECTIONS

Mix above ingredients into a smooth paste and set aside.

BROWNIE INGREDIENTS

3/4	Cup	Margarine
1	Cup	Brown sugar
1	Tbl	Cocoa
1	Tsp	Vanilla
1	Cup	Coconut
1	Cup	Rolled oats
1	Cup	Flour
1	Cup	Milk

DIRECTIONS

Put margarine, sugar, cocoa, and vanilla into a heavy saucepan on the asbestos pad on medium heat and stir until the margarine melts. Combine the dry ingredients and add to saucepan. Stir until mixture is hot and crisp. You may have to turn the flame up; it takes about 10 minutes for the mixture to become crisp. Add milk and stir constantly until the mixture is very hot and forms a ball in cold water.

Remove from stove and press mixture into the oiled pan with the back of a spoon. Spread on the icing immediately. Set aside to cool. When cold, cut into squares or bars.

Fried Peanut Bars
Roll in confectioners sugar and serve when cold

INGREDIENTS

1	Cup	Flour
1	Tsp	Baking powder
	Pinch	Salt
1/2	Cup	Sugar
1/4	Cup	Chopped peanuts
2	Tbls	Butter or margarine
1		Egg
4	Tbls	Milk
1	Tsp	Vanilla

DIRECTIONS

Sift the flour, salt, and baking powder into a bowl. Cut the butter into the flour mixture with a fork. Add peanuts and sugar. Add the egg and enough milk to make a stiff dough. Mix well; then turn out onto a well-floured board. Pat flat into a round about 3/4 inch thick. Cut into wedge-shaped bars. Makes 18.

In a heavy skillet put 3 tablespoons oil and heat until very hot. Turn the flame down and put the bars into the hot oil. Cook on one side, then turn over and cook on the other. Use low heat as it takes awhile to cook through. Remove when cooked and roll the bars in confectioners sugar.

VARIATIONS

Omit the peanuts and use raisins, cocoa, chopped walnuts, cherries, coconut, or other flavorings. If doubling the recipe, do not add extra egg.

PUDDINGS

*The proof of the pudding
  is the eating
    —Miguel De Cervantes*

Bread Pudding "Honnalee"
Cooked on top of the stove and poured into a mold to set

INGREDIENTS

2	Cups	Bread
3	Cups	Milk
4	Tbls	Custard powder
1	Tsp	Vanilla
1/2	Cup	Sugar
1	Cup	Raisins
1	Tbl	Oil

DIRECTIONS

Break bread into chunks and tightly fill 2 cups. Put into a bowl and add 1 cup of milk to moisten all the bread. Let this set while you mix together the remaining milk, custard powder, vanilla, sugar, and raisins. Pour mixture over bread and stir thoroughly.

Heat a heavy saucepan on the asbestos pad until the lid is too hot to touch. Pour oil into the hot pan and spread it up the sides. Pour the pudding mixture into the saucepan, put on the lid, turn the flame to low, and cook over the asbestos pad for 30 minutes.

Pour the mixture out of the saucepan into a bowl. It will look messy but will mold in the bowl. When cold, turn upside down onto a plate. Serve in slices, plain or with a sauce. The slices may be fried in butter on both sides and sprinkled with brown sugar.

Coconut and Jam Steamed Pudding

INGREDIENTS

1	Tbl	Butter (heaping)
2	Tbls	Coconut
	Pinch	Salt
2		Eggs
1	Cup	Flour
3/4	Cup	Sugar
4	Tbls	Milk
1	Tsp	Baking powder
3	Tbls	Jam

DIRECTIONS

Pour melted butter in a mixing bowl and add in the following order:
sugar, coconut, salt, milk, eggs and flour. Stir all gently together and beat
for 2 minutes. Stir in baking powder and mix well. Put jam into a greased
bowl and pour the batter over it. Cover with foil, place on a trivet in
saucepan partly filled with water, and steam for 1 1/2 hours. Check saucepan occasionally to see if more water is needed. Serve with vanilla custard sauce (see page 69).

Cottage Pudding

INGREDIENTS

1 3/4	Cups	Flour
3	Tsps	Baking powder
1/2	Tsp	Salt
1/4	Cup	Butter
1		Egg
1/2	Cup	Milk

DIRECTIONS

Cream the butter and sugar and add the salt and egg. Beat well. Sift the flour and baking powder and add alternately with milk. Spread a thick layer of sliced apples, peaches, pineapple, or other fruit mixture on the bottom of a well-greased bowl. Sprinkle with sugar and nutmeg. Pour the batter over the top and cover with foil. Steam for 45 minutes in a saucepan with a trivet on the bottom. The water should be three-fourths of the way up the pudding bowl at the beginning. Check to be sure it doesn't boil away. Add more water if necessary.

VARIATIONS

Add figs, currents, or dates to the batter.

Ginger Steamed Pudding

INGREDIENTS

1/2	Cup	Butter
4	Tbls	Sugar
2	Tbls	Corn syrup
1		Egg
1/2	Cup	Milk (approx.)
1	Cup	Flour
	Pinch	Salt
1	Tsp	Baking soda
1	Tsp	Ground ginger

DIRECTIONS

Cream butter, sugar, and corn syrup together. Add a beaten egg and mix well. Dissolve soda in the milk and add alternately with dry ingredients. Pour into a greased bowl and cover with foil. Steam in a saucepan partially filled with water for 2 hours. Serve with one of the basic dessert sauces (see page 69).

VARIATIONS

Add 4 tablespoons of raisins and 1 teaspoon chopped sugared ginger.

Sago Plum Pudding
A favorite Australian pudding.

INGREDIENTS

1/2	Cup	Sago
1 1/4	Cups	Milk
1	Tbl	Butter
1	Tsp	Baking soda
		Extra Milk
1 1/2	Cup	Soft white bread crumbs
1/2	Cup	Sugar
1 1/2	Cups	Seeded raisins
1/2	Tsp	Lemon essence

DIRECTIONS

Wash sago in cold water; then soak in the milk for at least 4 hours or overnight. Melt butter and add to the sago. Dissolve the soda in a little milk and add to the sago with the bread crumbs, sugar, raisins, and essence. Mix well. Pour the mixture into a well-greased pudding bowl. Cover with foil and steam for 2 1/2 hours in a saucepan. Watch the water level and don't let the pan boil dry. Add more water when necessary. Serve with custard sauce (see page 69-70).

New Zealand Steamed Pudding

INGREDIENTS

1	Cup	Flour
1	Tsp	Baking powder
4	Tbls	Butter
1/4	Cup	Sugar
1		Egg
1/2	Cup	Milk

DIRECTIONS

Sift the dry ingredients. Cream the butter and sugar together. Add the egg and beat well. Add the milk and dry ingredients alternately. Pour the mixture into a greased quart pudding bowl. Cover with foil and steam for 2 hours in a saucepan partially filled with water.

VARIATIONS

Arrange cooked, pitted prunes on bottom of the bowl. Add 1 teaspoon cinnamon to the dry ingredients. Put 1 cup stewed apples in the bottom of the bowl. Add 1/2 teaspoon ground cloves to dry ingredients. Add nutmeg and chopped dates to dry ingredients. Add raisins and grated orange rind to the dry ingredients. Add 4 tablespoons of syrup to bottom of the pudding bowl, cover with batter and steam. Serve with a basic dessert sauce (see page 69).

Lemon Steamed Pudding

INGREDIENTS

5/8	Cup	Flour
1	Tsp	Baking powder
1/2	Cup	Sugar
1/2		Lemon grated and juiced
6	Tbls	Butter
1	Large	Egg
3	Tbls	Milk

(continued)

DIRECTIONS

Sift the flour and baking powder into a bowl. Add the other ingredients
and beat well. When smooth, pour into a well-greased bowl and cover
with foil. Steam for 2 hours in a saucepan partially filled with water.
Serve with a basic dessert sauce (see page 69).

Hot Sherry Pudding
A fluffy pudding to serve

INGREDIENTS

5		Egg yolks
3/4	Cup	Sugar
1	Tbl	Cold water
		Dash of Salt
1/2	Cup	Sherry

DIRECTIONS

Beat the egg yolks and water in the top of a double boiler until they are
foamy. Beat in the sugar, salt, and sherry. Put pan over hot, not boiling,
water and beat the mixture until it thickens. This will only take a few
minutes. Serve hot.

VARIATIONS

Add grated chocolate to pudding when you remove from heat but don't
stir any more than necessary.

Add chopped walnuts and cherries.

Add shredded coconut.

Cold Sherry Pudding

INGREDIENTS

5		Eggs
1	Tbl	Cold water
3/4	Cup	Sugar
	Dash	Salt
1/2	Cup	Sherry

DIRECTIONS

Whisk the egg yolks and water in the top of a double boiler until foamy. Add sugar, salt, and sherry and beat well. Put pan over hot, not boiling, water and beat constantly until the mixture thickens; it thickens quickly. Set aside while you beat the egg whites until stiff. Add 1 tablespoon sugar and beat until peaked. Fold into the pudding, then set aside to cool.

VARIATIONS

Add chopped cherries before the egg whites.

Serve with berries or fresh fruit.

Sprinkle with chopped walnuts or pecans.

DESSERT SAUCES, CREAMS, CUSTARDS, AND FRUIT DESSERTS

Basic Dessert Sauce
Pour over steamed puddings

INGREDIENTS

1	Tbl	Corn starch
1/2	Cup	Sugar
	Pinch	Salt
1		Egg
2	Tbls	Butter
2	Tsps	Vanilla
1	Cup	Hot milk

DIRECTIONS

Mix the corn starch, sugar, and salt with a little water. Slowly add to the hot milk. Cook until thickened. Beat the egg and gradually add to the hot mixture, stirring constantly. Cook for 1 minute, remove from the flame, and add butter and vanilla.

VARIATIONS

Use 1 cup of water instead of milk. Omit vanilla and add 2 tablespoons of lemon juice and 1 teaspoon grated lemon rind.

Add 1/2 teaspoon grated nutmeg to the above recipe.

Add a scant tablespoon of cocoa to the corn starch mixture.

Custard and Cream
An easy dessert to make

INGREDIENTS

2	Cups	Milk
2	Tbls	Sugar (level)
1		Egg
		Pinch of salt
2	Tbls	Corn starch (scant)
		Small container of cream

DIRECTIONS

Heat the milk slowly to the boiling point and add sugar. Beat the egg with a pinch of salt and mix in corn starch that has been moistened with milk. Dribble the corn starch mixture slowly into the hot milk, stirring constantly until it thickens. Set aside to cool. When quite cold, beat in the cream until smooth. Serve plain or over fruit or cake.

Exotic Things with Custard Powder

INGREDIENTS

1	Package	Custard
1	Tbl	Butter or margarine (heaping)
		Handful of raisins
1		Apple
1	Tbl	Sugar
1/4	Cup	Rum or brandy

DIRECTIONS

Make custard as directed on the package and set aside to cool.

Heat butter or margarine in a small skillet. Add raisins and apple, which has been cored and cut into cubes. Sprinkle sugar over top of the fruit and stir fry until apple is tender. Remove from heat and pour rum or brandy over the fruit. Reheat gently until brandy or rum is just warm. Remove from the flame and ignite.

(continued)

After the rum or brandy has burnt and the flame is out, add the fruit mixture to the custard. Pour into individual serving dishes and cool.

VARIATIONS

Put a layer of custard in individual sherbert glasses; then a layer of rum-fruit mixture, then another layer of custard. Top with whipped cream or cream topping and put a marachino cherry on top.

Mock Cream

INGREDIENTS

3/4	Cup	Water
3	Tbls	Powdered milk
3	Tbls	Corn Starch
5	Tbls	Confectioners sugar
1 1/2	Tbls	Butter or margarine

DIRECTIONS

Mix the corn starch with 3 tablespoons of water. Heat the rest of the water and powdered milk just to the boiling point. Gradually pour the corn starch into the hot milk, stirring constantly so it doesn't become lumpy. The mixture will become very thick. Cook for 1 minute and set aside to cool.

Cream the sugar and butter until smooth. Add the corn starch mixture, one teaspoon at a time, and beat well between each addition. When there is enough in the bowl, use a beater. When all the mixture has been added, beat in the vanilla. Fill brandy snaps or curls or use between layers of cakes.

VARIATIONS

Add any of the following after the vanilla: coconut, chopped walnuts, finely grated orange or lemon rind, or small chips of chocolate.

72

Cream Filling

INGREDIENTS

1	Cup	Milk
1/4	Cup	Sugar
2	Tbls	Corn starch
	Dash	Salt
1		Egg
1/2	Tbl	Butter

DIRECTIONS

Scald milk in the top of a double boiler. Mix sugar, corn starch and salt.
Stir into the milk. Keep stirring until it becomes thick. Then cover and
cook for 10 minutes longer. Add a small amount of the mixture to a beaten
egg, then return the egg mixture to the custard mixture, stirring all the time.
Cook for 5 minutes. Add butter, mix well, pour into a bowl, and sprinkle a
small amount of sugar over the top to prevent a skin from forming. Chill and
fill brandy snaps or caramel curls or use in layer cakes.

VARIATIONS

Add 3/4 teaspoon vanilla, or add 2 teaspoons cocoa to sugar.

Peaches Aflame
Brandy on sugar cubes

INGREDIENTS

Fresh ripe peaches
Sugar-syrup (2 parts sugar, 1 part water)
Sugar cubes
Brandy

DIRECTIONS

Wash peaches and dip into boiling water just long enough to blanch.
Remove the skins, halve, and remove the stones. Boil the sugar and
water until sugar is dissolved. Poach peaches in this syrup until just tender. Remove and arrange on a heatproof dish. Place a sugar cube on each
half. Pour a little warmed brandy over the sugar cubes. When ready to

(continued)

serve, ignite the brandy. A faintly caramel flavor will be added to the peaches.

VARIATIONS

When using canned fruit, just heat the fruit in its juice and follow the above procedure. Apricots, pineapple, pawpaw, or pears can be treated the same way.

Apricot Cheesecake
Use a vanilla instant pudding powder

INGREDIENTS (Crust)

2	Cups	Cookie crumbs
1/2	Tsp	Ground ginger
6	Tbls	Melted butter

DIRECTIONS

Combine the above ingredients, press mixture into an 8-inch pie plate, and set aside to cool.

INGREDIENTS (Filling)

1 1/2	Cups	Cream cheese
1/2	Cup	Milk
1	Package	Vanilla instant pudding powder

1 16-ounce can of apricot pieces or 2 cans pureed apricots (baby food), enough to make 1 cup of pureed apricots.

DIRECTIONS

Soften the cream cheese in the milk and add one cup pureed apricots. Sprinkle the instant pudding powder on top and beat until nearly set. Pour on top of pie shell and set aside to set or put in refrigerator to chill.

Fried Bananas and Raspberry Sauce
Good when bananas are plentiful

INGREDIENTS

5		Bananas
2	Tbls	Flour
1		Egg
1	Cup	Wafer crumbs
		Oil for frying
1/2	Cup	Rasberry jam
		Juice of 1 lemon
		Hot water
1	Tsp	Corn starch
		Oil for frying

DIRECTIONS

Coat peeled bananas in flour, dip in a beaten egg, and roll in crumbs. Fry in oil until crumbs are crisp and lightly browned.

SAUCE

Add the lemon juice to half cup of rasberry jam and enough water to fill the cup. Bring to a boil and thicken with the corn starch mixed in a little water. Pour hot over the fried bananas. Add whipped cream or a topping if you wish.

Apple Delight
Bread crumbs, brown sugar, apples, and cream

INGREDIENTS

1	Cup	Brown bread crumbs
1/2	Cup	Brown Sugar
1/4	Cup	Butter
2	Cups	Apples, peeled and sliced
		Juice from 1 lemon
		Dash of cinnamon
		Sugar to taste
1	Cup	Cream

(continued)

DIRECTIONS

Mix bread crumbs, brown sugar, and butter together in a skillet and cook until sugar is melted and the crumbs are a golden brown. Set aside to cool.

Cook apples, lemon juice, cinnamon, and sugar together until apples are tender. Set aside to cool. Beat cream until it peaks. Add a little sugar to taste.

Place a layer of apples in a serving dish and top with a layer of bread crumbs. Continue to make layers until all the apples and bread crumbs are used. Top with whipped cream and sprinkle with chopped nuts or grated chocolate.

VARIATIONS

Add 1/4 cup of chopped walnuts to the crumb mixture.

Add 1/4 cup raisins to the apples while cooking.

You can use canned apples and any whipped topping instead of cream.

Toffee Apple Dessert
Whole apples cooked in the skillet

INGREDIENTS

1/2	Cup	Molasses
1/2	Cup	Sugar
3	Tbls	Lemon juice
1/2	Cup	Water
6		Tart cooking apples
1	Pint	Ice cream

DIRECTIONS

Mix the molasses, sugar, water, and lemon juice in a 10-inch skillet. Bring to a boil, add the peeled and cored apples, and reduce the heat. Cover and cook for 15 minutes. Uncover, turn the apples over, and simmer for another 20 minutes, or until the apples are tender. With a sharp knife cut each apple into petals but not all the way through. Lift each apple out of skillet into individual serving dishes and top with a small scoop of ice cream just before serving. Pour the remaining syrup over ice cream. If ice cream is not available, use a whipped topping or whipped cream.

Fruit and Nut Pancake
Use chopped apples or peaches with nuts and raisins

INGREDIENTS

2	Tbls	Butter or margarine
		Chopped apples or peaches
1/2	Cup	Chopped nuts
1/2	Cup	Raisins
1/2	Cup	Brown sugar
		Cinnamon
1		Egg
1/2	Cup	Milk
2	Tbls	Flour
1	Tsp	Oil
1	Tsp	Sugar
		Dash of salt

DIRECTIONS

Melt butter or margarine in a skillet. Add enough chopped apples or peaches to cover the bottom. Stir fry until the fruit is slightly browned. Add nuts and raisins and sprinkle with cinnamon and brown sugar. Cook until fruit is caramelized, but don't let it burn.

Beat an egg in a bowl and add milk, flour, oil, sugar, and salt. Mix well into a smooth batter. Pour over the hot fruit and cook for 12 minutes with lid on the skillet over low heat, or until batter is cooked.

Egg Dishes

Look at an egg and see what a delicate thing it is. Cook it gently, over low heat, if you want your egg dishes to be successful.

Egg Cutlets
Dipped in egg and bread crumbs and fried

INGREDIENTS

5		Eggs
2	Tbls	Butter
2	Tbls	Flour (scant)
		Pinch of salt
		Pepper
		Parsley
		Bread crumbs

DIRECTIONS

Boil 4 eggs until hard. When cold, peel them and rub them through a fine sieve or chop very fine.

Put butter and flour in a saucepan. Cook over low heat for 5 minutes, stirring all the time. Mix with the eggs. Add salt, pepper, and chopped parsley. Set aside to cool.

When cold, form into cutlets and dip into a well-beaten egg and then into bread crumbs. Fry very quickly in boiling fat or hot bubbly butter. Makes 8 small cutlets.

VARIATION

Chop up prawns, crab, or chicken and use instead of hard-boiled eggs.

Asparagus, Poached Egg and Cheese
Cheesy sauce over pouched eggs for lunch

INGREDIENTS

1	Can	Asparagus
4		Eggs
2	Tbls	Butter
2	Tbls	Flour
1	Cup	Milk
1/2	Cup	Grated cheese

DIRECTIONS

Gently heat asparagus and keep hot while preparing sauce. Heat butter, add flour, and cook for 3 minutes. Add milk slowly, stirring all the time. Add cheese and cook 2 minutes. Leave warming. Poach eggs and make 4 rounds of toast. Put toast on serving plates, butter, and add asparagus. Lay a poached egg on top. Pour cheese sauce over the eggs. Sprinkle with a little cayenne pepper and granish with parsley. Serves 4.

Eggs à la Suisse
Sherry and cream sauce

INGREDIENTS

1	Tbl	Butter
1/2	Cup	Cream
4		Eggs
		Salt and pepper to taste
		Sherry

DIRECTIONS

Melt butter in a skillet. Add cream. Add 4 eggs, one at a time, and be careful not to break the yolks. Season with salt and pepper or sprinkle a dash of paprika, cayenne pepper, or curry powder over the eggs. Put on the lid and gently cook until whites are firm. Mix a little sherry in some cream and pour over the eggs. Serve on buttered toast.

Eggs in Red Wine
Poached eggs with wine sauce

INGREDIENTS

1	Cup	Red wine
1/2	Cup	Water
1/2	Bay leaf	
	Pinch	Thyme, parsley, or oregano
		Salt and pepper to taste
4		Eggs
1/2	Tbl	Butter
1/2	Tbl	Flour

DIRECTIONS

Mix the wine, water, and herbs in a saucepan and simmer for 5 minutes. Then poach eggs in the wine mixture. Place eggs on buttered toast and keep warm.

SAUCE

Add butter that has been mixed into a paste with 1/2 tablespoon flour to the wine mixture. Stir and cook until the sauce is thick and then spoon over each egg.

Cheesy Eggs
They have a touch of onion

INGREDIENTS

1	Small	Onion chopped fine
2	Tbls	Butter
3/4	Cup	Water
1/2	Cup	Grated cheese
6		Eggs slightly beaten
		Salt and pepper to taste

DIRECTIONS

Saute the onions in butter until golden brown. Mix the water, cheese, and eggs together. Add salt and pepper and pour over the onions. Cook over low heat until the desired consistency, stirring constantly. Serve on buttered toast.

Eggs with a Difference
Onion, tomato, and eggs on toast

INGREDIENTS

1		Onion
1	Small	Garlic clove
1	Tsp	Olive Oil
3-4		Tomatoes
		Salt and pepper
		Pinch cayenne pepper
1		Red pepper
1		Green pepper
3		Eggs

DIRECTIONS

Put the olive oil into the skillet and saute the chopped and crushed garlic. Add peeled tomatoes, seasoning, and chopped peppers to the onion mixture. Cover and simmer until soft and pulpy. Beat the eggs slightly and spread evenly over the pulpy mixture. Cover again and simmer for 10 minutes to set the eggs. Serve on hot, buttered toast.

Hot Curried Egg Sauce
Serve over rice or on hot toast

INGREDIENTS

4		Hardboiled eggs
1	8-ounce	Can tomato puree
1/2	Tsp	Hot curry powder
1/2	Tsp	Salt
1	Tbl	Butter

DIRECTIONS

Add the seasoning and butter to the puree in a saucepan and gently cook until the puree thickens. Carefully add the sliced eggs. Heat thoroughly. Serve over hot cooked rice or on hot buttered toast.

Poached Eggs in Tomato Sauce
A Greek recipe with fresh tomatoes and cinnamon

INGREDIENTS

3-4	Large	Tomatoes
1		Garlic clove
		Good dash cinnamon
2	Tbls	Butter
1/4	Tsp	Sugar
		Salt and pepper to taste
3-4		Eggs

DIRECTIONS

Peel and chop finely the tomatoes and cook in a saucepan with crushed garlic, butter, and cinnamon. Add sugar, salt, and pepper. Mix well. Drop the eggs into the hot sauce and poach them adding enough water to cover the eggs. Serve on buttered toast. Pour a little of the sauce over the eggs.

Spanish Eggs and Tuna
Tuna, green peppers, onions, and eggs

INGREDIENTS

2	Tbls	Olive oil
1		Chopped onion
1		Green pepper chopped
8		Eggs
1	8-ounce	Can tuna
1/2	Tsp	Salt
		Pepper to taste

DIRECTIONS

Pour olive oil into a skillet and saute the onions and green peppers for 5 minutes. Beat the eggs until creamy. Add salt, pepper, and chunked tuna. Pour over the vegetables. Cook. Lift the edges with a spatula to allow uncooked egg to run underneath. Cut into wedges and turn each wedge over to brown. Serve with hot buttered toast. Serves 4.

Tangy Creamed Eggs
Hard-boiled eggs in hot tangy sauce

INGREDIENTS

1/4	Cup	Butter
1/4	Cup	Flour
1	Tsp	Worchestershire sauce
1 1/2	Cups	Milk
1/2	Cup	Cream
	Dash	Tabasco sauce
2	Tbls	Chopped parsley
1		Chopped green pepper (optional)
8	.	Hard-boiled eggs
		Salt and pepper to taste

DIRECTIONS

Melt the butter in a saucepan and mix in the flour. Add the milk and cream. (Use powdered milk and make 2 cups with extra powder instead of the cream.) Cook and stir until sauce thickens. Add Worchestershire and tabasco sauce, chopped parsley, and green peppers. stir until mixed, then gently add the sliced hard-boiled eggs. Just heat. Season with salt and pepper and serve with hot, buttered toast.

Top-of-The-Stove-Egg-Pie
"Honnalee's" Red Sea recipe — Easy full meal when seas are rough

INGREDIENTS

Bacon, ham or luncheon meat
2 Onions or leeks
Can of diced potatoes
Eggs

DIRECTIONS

Chop bacon, ham or luncheon meat into cubes. Place in a skillet and brown. Add chopped onions or leeks and potatoes. Stir fry until piping hot. Break enough eggs over the top to feed the hungry crew. Cover with lid and cook slowly until eggs are set. Serve piping hot with salad, bread, and butter.

Cheese Dishes

Cheese Fritters
Raw potato and grated cheese

INGREDIENTS

1 1/2	Cups	Grated potato
1/2	Cup	Grated cheese
2		Eggs
2	Tsps	Chopped onions
1	Cup	Milk
1/2	Tsp	Salt
1/2	Cup	Flour
		Pepper

DIRECTIONS

Separate the eggs and beat the whites until stiff. Beat the yolks until creamy and add milk, salt, and pepper. Stir in sifted flour. Add the grated potatoes, cheese, and onion. Fold in the stiffly beaten egg whites. Drop by tablespoons into hot oil and fry until golden brown.

84

Quick Cheesy Supper
Instant mashed potatoes and cheese

INGREDIENTS

1	Package	Instant mashed potatoes
2		Eggs
1/2	Cup	Grated cheese
1	Tsp	Hot mustard
		Salt and pepper
2	Tbls	Melted butter

DIRECTIONS

Make the mashed potatoes according to the directions on the package. Add well-beaten eggs and grated cheese. Mix in the mustard and seasoning. Melt butter in a skillet and add the mixture, spreading it evenly over the bottom. Cook on low heat until the under side is brown. Cut into wedges and turn each wedge over to brown. Serve with leftover meat or fresh green salad. You can also make individual patties out of the mixture.

Cheese and Potatoes
A tasty dish using leftover potatoes

INGREDIENTS

About 5		Leftover potatoes
2		Eggs
3/4	Cup	Grated cheese
1	Tsp	Hot mustard
2	Tbls	Butter
		Salt and pepper to taste

DIRECTIONS

Cut the potatoes into bite-size pieces. Add the grated cheese, eggs, salt, and pepper. Add the mustard mixed with a little water. Melt butter in a skillet and add the prepared mixture. Fry for 5-6 minutes until the mixture is golden brown underneath. Gently cut into wedges and turn the wedges over to brown on the other side. Serve with salad for lunch.

Mexican Rarebit
Serve on toast for lunch

INGREDIENTS

2	Tbls	Butter
1		Green pepper
3/4	Cup	Grated cheese
4	oz	Can kernel corn
1	Medium	Tomato
1/4	Cup	Bread crumbs
1		Egg
		Salt and pepper

DIRECTIONS

Melt the butter in a saucepan and add a seeded and sliced green pepper. Stew gently until soft. Add the cheese and stir until it has melted. Beat the egg and stir into the mixture with the corn, bread crumbs and a chopped tomato. Season with salt and pepper. Stir well to mix. Serve on slices of buttered toast.

Mock Whitebait Patties
Use grated potato and cheese

INGREDIENTS

2 1/2	Tbls	Flour
1		Egg
2	Tbls	Milk
3	Tbls	.Grated cheese (heaping)
1	Medium	Potato, grated
1	Tsp	Baking powder
		Pepper and salt to taste

DIRECTIONS

Beat the egg and add the flour, milk, cheese, and seasoning. Add a grated potato and baking powder just before frying. Heat about 1/2 inch oil in a skillet and fry patties for about 5 minutes on each side. Serve hot and garnish with parsley.

Wine Sandwich
Cheesy wine sandwich for lunch

INGREDIENTS

2		Eggs
2	Tbls	Milk
1	Jigger	Sherry or wine
3	Shakes	Worchestershire sauce

DIRECTIONS

Beat the eggs slightly and mix in milk, sherry or wine, and Worchestershire sauce. Make a cheese sandwich and dip it in the mixture. Fry the sandwich in an oiled skillet until brown on one side, then turn over and fry the other side. Cook until cheese melts. Serve with salad for lunch.

Macaroni and Cheese
Top with browned bread crumbs

INGREDIENTS

1	8-ounce	Package elbow macaroni
4	Tbls	Butter
1/4	Cup	Flour
1	Small	Onion, grated
1	Tbl	Worchestershire sauce
1	Cup	Bread crumbs
		Butter to brown
3	Tsps	Prepared mustard or 1 tsp. dry mustard
1	Tsp	Salt
2 1/2	Cups	Milk
1	Pound	Grated cheese

DIRECTIONS

Cook macaroni, following the directions on the package. Drain and spoon into a serving dish and keep warm.

Melt the butter in a medium-size saucepan, stir in flour, onion, Worchestershire sauce, mustard, and salt. Cook and constantly stir until mixture is just bubbling. Stir in milk and continue stirring until sauce thickens and boils. Add the cheese, remove from the stove, and stir until cheese just melts. Pour the macaroni into the cheese mixture. Stir lightly to mix. Keep warm until ready to serve.

Brown bread crumbs in enough butter to coat them well. Pour the macaroni into a serving dish and sprinkle the browned bread crumbs over the top.

Macaroni, Cheese, and Onions
A sauce for macaroni that is different

INGREDIENTS

1	Package	Elbow macaroni
3		Medium-sized onions
2	Tbls	Butter
1	Cup	Grated cheese
		Water

DIRECTIONS

Cook macaroni according to directions on the package. Peel onions and slice very thin. Put butter into a saucepan and when hot and melted, add the onions. Saute until the onions are golden brown.Add grated cheese and stir until it melts. Pour over the cooked macaroni and serve.

Chicken Dishes

Chicken and Dumplings

INGREDIENTS

2-3	Lb	Fryer
1 1/2	Cups	Flour
1/4	Cup	Cornmeal
1	Tsp	Salt
		Pepper to taste
1	Tsp	Accent
1/2	Cup	Vegetable oil
1/4	Cup	Butter
3 1/2	Cups	Warm water

DIRECTIONS

Cut the chicken into portion-sized pieces. Mix flour, cornmeal, salt, pepper, and Accent together in a paper bag. Dredge the chicken pieces with the flour in the bag. Put the oil in a skillet and brown chicken on all sides. Pour off any excess oil. Remove the chicken.

Put the butter and warm water into the skillet. When butter is melted, place the browned chicken pieces into the mixture. Simmer covered for 30-40 minutes. As soon as the chicken is tender, top with dumplings. Cover and cook 15 minutes longer. Do not lift the lid during the 15 minutes.

Dumplings

1	Cup	Flour
1	Tsp	Baking powder
1/2	Tsp	Salt
1	Tbl	Chopped onion
1/8	Tsp	Ground nutmeg
2		Egg yolks
1/2	Cup	Milk

DIRECTIONS

Sift flour and baking powder together. Add salt and onions. Mix well and add nutmeg. Beat 2 egg yolks until creamy. Add alternately with milk. Drop by teaspoons into the hot chicken mixture. Cook covered for 15 minutes.

Noodle Chicken
Simmer in three soups and topped with crisp noodles

INGREDIENTS

1		Frying chicken or chicken pieces
1/2	Can	Mushroom soup
1/2	Can	Chicken creamed soup
1/2	Cup	Milk
1/2	Package	Onion soup
1	Can	Chow mein noodles
		Flour, salt, and pepper

DIRECTIONS

Cut the chicken into portion-size pieces. Sprinkle with seasoned flour. Heat enough oil in a skillet to brown the chicken. Pour off any excess oil when chicken is browned. Add the three soups that have been mixed with milk and seasoned to taste. Cover and simmer until the chicken is cooked and tender. Check occasionally to make sure the sauce isn't too thick. When chicken is cooked, remove the lid and cook until the sauce becomes thick. Serve with crisp chow mein noodles sprinkled over the sauce.

Chicken Oregano
A meal in a skillet with a Greek Flavor

INGREDIENTS

1		Frying chicken
1/2	Cup	Olive Oil
		Salt and pepper to taste
2	Tsps	Oregano
2		Chicken cubes
1/2	Cup	Water
4		Onions
4		Potatoes

(continued)

DIRECTIONS

Cut a frying chicken into serving-size portions. Heat olive oil in a skillet and when it is hot, brown the chicken pieces. Pour off the excess oil. Sprinkle the chicken with salt, pepper, and oregano.

Dissolve chicken cubes in water and pour over the chicken. Arrange sliced onions and peeled and quartered potatoes around the chicken pieces. Cover and simmer for 30 minutes, or until the chicken and vegetables are tender.

Fried Chicken with Pineapple
Paprika and pineapple give the flavor

INGREDIENTS

1		Frying chicken
1/2	Cup	Flour
1/4	Tsp	Salt
	Dash	Pepper
1/2	Tsp	Paprika
4	Tbls	Butter
1	Can	Pineapple chunks and juice

DIRECTIONS

Cut the chicken up into portion-size pieces. Mix the salt, pepper, flour and paprika and dredge the chicken pieces in them. Melt the butter in a large skillet and arrange the chicken so it will brown evenly. When the chicken is golden brown, add the pineapple chunks and the juice. Cover and cook on medium heat for about 25 minutes or until the chicken is tender. Remove the cover and cook for an additional 10 minutes to reduce the liquid and crisp the chicken. Place the chicken on a platter and pour any extra gravy over it. Garnish with parsley and sliced tomatoes. Serve with mashed potatoes or rice.

Chicken in Marjoram Butter
Pecans and small potatoes complete the dish

INGREDIENTS

1		Frying chicken
1/4	Cup	Margarine
1/4	Tsp	Marjoram
		Flour
		Salt and pepper
1/2	Cup	Shelled pecans
		Small cooked potatoes

DIRECTIONS

Cut the chicken into portion-size pieces and dredge in seasoned flour. Heat the margarine in a skillet and add the marjoram. Brown the chicken pieces, cover, and cook on low heat for 40-50 minutes. When chicken is tender, add the pecans and small cooked potatoes. Serve when hot.

Chicken in Sage-and-Mushroom Gravy
Skillet cooked chicken

INGREDIENTS

2	Tbls	Margarine
1		Frying chicken
1	Can	Cream mushroom soup
1	Tsp	Sage
1/2	Tsp	Salt
	Dash	Pepper
1/4	Cup	Water

DIRECTIONS

Cut the chicken into portion-size pieces. Heat the margarine in a skillet and brown the chicken. Turn to brown on all sides. Mix water with the mushroom soup. Add sage, salt, and pepper. Pour over the chicken. Cover with a lid and simmer for 40 minutes until the chicken is cooked. Serves four.

Chicken Stewed in Mushroom Soup

INGREDIENTS

1	3-4 lb	Stewing chicken
1	Cup	Flour
		Salt and pepper
1/2	Cup	Oil
1	Can	Mushroom soup
1/2	Cup	Evaporated milk or equivalent
1	Cup	Sliced onions
1/4	Tsp	Thyme
1/8	Tsp	Savory

DIRECTIONS

Cut the chicken into portion-size pieces and roll in flour that has been seasoned with salt and pepper. Put oil in a skillet and brown the chicken pieces. Pour off any excess oil. Mix the soup with the milk and pour over the chicken. Sprinkle with thyme and savory. Bring the mixture to a slow simmer and cook for 40-50 minutes or until the chicken is cooked. Serves four.

VARIATIONS

Add peas just before serving

Add niblet style corn just before serving.

Chicken Livers Smothered in Onions

INGREDIENTS

1	lb	Chicken livers
		Salt and pepper to taste
1/4	Cup	Margarine
2	Cups	Onions
1	Can	Whole mushrooms

DIRECTIONS

Cut the livers into pieces and season with salt and pepper. Melt the mar-
over low heat for 10
minutes. Remove the cover and add the drained can of mushrooms. Cover
and cook for another 5 minutes. Remove the cover and turn the heat up
slightly. Brown while turning the mixture. Serve hot on buttered toast or
with potatoes and vegetables. Serves four.

Chicken Livers with Wild Rice

INGREDIENTS

1	lb	Chicken livers
1/4	Cup	Butter
1/2	Cup	Diced bacon or bacon bits
1/4	Cup	Chopped onion
1/4	Cup	Chopped celery
1	Cup	Mushroom buttons
3		Pimientos, cubed
3	Cups	Cooked wild rice
1/2	Tsp	Salt

DIRECTIONS

Cut the chicken livers in half and melt the margarine in a skillet. Saute
the bacon until crisp, then remove from pan and set aside. Put the chicken
livers in the margarine and bacon fat and saute until tender. Remove the
livers and set aside. Put the onions and celery into the skillet and saute
until tender. Return the bacon and livers to the skillet. Add the mushrooms and pimientos. Cook for 5 minutes. Stir in cooked wild rice and
salt. When hot, serve. Serves four.

Stuffed Chicken Pot Roast Style

INGREDIENTS

1		Roasting chicken
		Stuffing
		Salt and pepper
3/4	Cup	Water
		Potatoes, halved
		Carrots cut into sticks
		Onions sliced
1	Can	Mushrooms
1	Can	Green peas or beans
		Vegetable oil

DIRECTIONS

Fill the chicken with stuffing and sew up and tie the legs together. Brown in a heavy saucepan in vegetable oil. Pour off any excess oil. Remove the chicken, put a trivit rack into the saucepan, and place the chicken on top. Pour in the water. Season with salt and pepper. Cover and simmer for 1 hour.

Add the vegetables, except the peas and mushrooms, and simmer for 30 minutes or until the potatoes are cooked. Add the drained peas and mushrooms and just heat. Remove the chicken to a platter. Put the vegetables around it and make gravy from the juice in the pot. Pour off any excess fat first. Thicken with flour and add water if necessary

(continued)

STUFFING

2	Cups	Onions
1	Tsp	Sage
1/2	Tsp	Thyme
1	Tsp	Salt
1/4	Tsp	Pepper
3	Cups	Stale bread crumbs
1/2	Cup	Chicken broth or water

DIRECTIONS

Moisten the bread crumbs with the broth or water. Chop onions finely and saute in butter. Add them and the rest of the ingredients to the bread crumbs and mix well. Stuff the chicken.

Chicken and Almonds
A very tasty Chinese dish from Singapore

INGREDIENTS

2	Cups	Chicken meat, raw
1	Tbl	Corn starch
1	Tsp	Salt
		Sprinkle of ground ginger
1/2	Cup	Onions or finely chopped leeks, the green stems for color
		Oil for deep frying
1	Cup	Blanched almonds
1/2	Cup	Stock
1	Tsp	Soy sauce
1	Tsp	Extra of corn starch
1	Tbl	Cold water
1	Cup	Canned bamboo shoots
1	Can	Mushrooms

DIRECTIONS

Mix the corn starch, salt, and ginger. Roll the chicken, diced into small pieces, in the mixture and toss to coat. Chop the onions, mushrooms, and bamboo shoots into small bite-size pieces.

(continued)

Heat oil in frying pan and fry almonds. When brown, remove and drain. Fry chicken pieces until golden and remove and drain. Pour off all but 2 tablespoons of oil and add the vegetables. Stir fry over high heat for 1 minute. Add the stock. Mix soy sauce and extra corn starch with cold water, add to the pan and allow to thicken. Add chicken pieces and heat through. Turn off heat and add almonds. Serve at once with rice or noodles.

VARIATIONS

Use salted almonds, peanuts, or walnuts instead of blanched almonds for a nice change.

Southern Fried Chicken
Creamy gravy surrounds this chicken dish

INGREDIENTS

1	2-3 pound	Frying chicken
1/2	Tsp	Salt
		Pepper to taste
1/2	Cup	Flour
1/2	Cup	Water
1/2	Cup	Cream
1/2	Cup	Peas
		Vegetable oil

DIRECTIONS

Cut the chicken into portion-size pieces. Roll them in a flour mixture that has been seasoned. Fry in hot vegetable oil until chicken is browned on all sides. Add water and put the lid on the skillet. Simmer for 20 minutes. Add peas and slowly stir in the cream. Heat until just boiling. If not thick enough for gravy, add a little flour mixed with water. Simmer, do not boil, for another 5 minutes.

Rice and Chicken Chop Chop

INGREDIENTS

1-2	Cups	Cooked chicken
1		Onion
1/2	Cup	Green beans
1/2	Cup	Celery
1/4	Tsp	Salt
		Pepper to taste
2	Tbls	Salad oil
1/2	Cup	Green pepper
1/2	Cup	Peeled tomatoes
3/4	Cup	Chicken stock
2	Tbls	Corn starch
1/4	Cup	Water
2	Tbls	Soy sauce
		Boiled rice for 4

DIRECTIONS

Chop chicken and all the vegetables before cooking. Heat in a skillet and stir fry the onions, beans, celery, and peppers for a few minutes. Add the chicken and tomatoes. Cook for a few minutes longer, then add the stock. Bring to a boil. Mix the corn starch with water, salt, pepper, and soy sauce in a small bowl. Stir into the boiling vegetables. Cook until the sauce thickens. Serve with fluffy rice.

Canned Meat Dishes

Corn beef, luncheon meats, and other little helpers make hamburgers, sausages, stews, enchiladas, pizzas, curried dinners, chili beans, and numerous other dishes.

Suggestions for Using Canned Meats.

Here are a few ways to camouflage the taste of canned meats and to enhance their flavor.

Canned Meat and Gravy

Add a good tablespoon of butter and a little salt and pepper to the meat while it is heating.

Meat Chunks

If a recipe calls for meat chunks, open a can of meat and gravy and drain off the gravy. Put meat into a sieve and rinse in cold water. Then you can fry the meat in butter until it is crisp. Use instead of fresh meat but add to recipe last as meat is already cooked.

Ham

Rinse ham in cold water before slicing to get rid of the preservative taste.

Corn Beef

Use corn beef in sandwiches, as fillings for enchiladas, in tortillas, pizzas, hashes, sliced and fried with eggs, patties, spaghetti, and a host of other dishes.

Steak and Onions

Because it is usually hashed in the can, use it for chili beans, sauces, and stews. Eliminate the onion in the recipe when using canned meat with onions.

Hamburgers

Made from canned meats, onions, mushroom soup, and seasoning

INGREDIENTS

1/4	Cup	Finely chopped onion
1/4	Tsp	Poultry seasoning
		Breadcrumbs
		Salt and pepper to taste
1	12-ounce	Can luncheon meat
1	5-ounce	Can turkey or chicken
1	Can	Creamed mushroom soup
1		Egg

DIRECTIONS

Slice luncheon meat and turkey and put through a course grinder or mash well. Add egg and 1/4 cup undiluted mushroom soup, onions, salt, pepper, and poultry seasoning. Form into thick patties and roll in bread crumbs. Fry until golden brown on each side and heated through. Serve with chips or on hamburger buns with lettuce and tomatoes.

Ravioli

Little meat-filled squares in tomato sauce

Pasta

INGREDIENTS

3/4	Cup	Flour
1		Egg
		Little water

DIRECTIONS

Make a paste of the above and knead until firm. Let set for 30 minutes.

(continued)

Sauce

INGREDIENTS

2	Tbls	Margarine
1 1/2	Cups	Water
1		Onion, chopped
1		Bouillon cube
4	Tsps	Sugar
2	Tbls	Olive oil (scant)
2	Tbls	Flour
		Bacon rinds
1	Can	Tomato puree
		Salt and pepper

DIRECTIONS

Mix the above ingredients, except sugar and seasoning, together in a saucepan and cook until thickened. Add sugar and seasoning.

Roll out pasta dough until thin and cut into 2-inch squares. Mix minced meat with gravy or a beaten egg, milk, and seasoning. Spoon this filling onto a pasta square. Place another square on top, dampen edges, and pinch together. When all the squares are filled, plunge them into briskly boiling water and let them cook for 8-10 minutes. Serve them hot with the tomato sauce poured over the top. Sprinkle with grated cheese.

Canned Meat Stew
Sweet basil enhances the flavor

INGREDIENTS

1	Large	Onion
1	Tbl	Butter
1	Tbl	Sweet basil
1	Small can	Diced carrots
1/2	Can	Drained peas
1	Can	Whole tomatoes
1	Can	New potatoes
1	Can	Meat, any kind
		Salt and pepper to taste

DIRECTIONS

Saute a diced onion in butter and add sweet basil. Stir fry for a few seconds. Add the rest of the ingredients and heat until boiling. Turn the burner down and simmer for 10 minutes. If stew is too thin, thicken with a little corn starch mixed with water.

You can use the following feather light dumpling recipe with this stew but add dumplings as soon as the stew boils.

Feather Light Dumplings
Don't lift the lid while dumplings are cooking

INGREDIENTS

1	Cup	Flour
2	Tsps	Baking powder
1		Egg
1	Tsp	Salt
2	Tbls	Butter
1/2	Cup	Milk

DIRECTIONS

Sift the dry ingredients together. Add egg, melted butter, and enough milk to make a stiff batter. Drop by tablespoons into the hot stew. Cover and cook 15-20 minutes. Do not lift the lid until cooking time is up or dumplings will be tough.

(continued)

Flavor the dumplings by adding one of the following:

2 Tbls Chopped parsley, 2 Tbls chopped chives, or Small Tsp mixed herbs.

Luncheon Meat and Noodles
Sliced meat, tangy sauce, and noodles

DIRECTIONS

Slice luncheon meat and dredge in seasoned flour. Fry lightly on both sides in butter. Add finely chopped onion. Cover with the following sauce and cook until thickened.

Sauce

INGREDIENTS

1/4	Tsp	Hot mustard mixed with water
3/4	Cup	Sour cream, or evaporated milk
2	Tbls	Vinegar (scant)
1	Small can	Tomato puree
1	Cup	Beef stock
	Dash	Worchestershire sauce

DIRECTIONS

Cook the tomato puree, beef stock, and seasonings for a few minutes until the sauce thickens. Add the sour cream and mix well. (If you don't have sour cream, mix three-fourths of a small can of evaporated milk with 2 scant tablespoons of vinegar). Heat and serve over noodles.

Corn Beef Patties
Corn beef fried in batter

INGREDIENTS

1		Egg
2	Tbls	Flour
1/2	Tsp	Baking powder
		Salt and pepper to taste
1/4	Tsp	Paprika
1	Can	Corn beef

DIRECTIONS

Mix the egg, flour, baking powder, salt, pepper, and paprika into a stiff batter. Slice the corn beef and dip into the batter. Fry in butter in a skillet until browned on both sides. Serve with potatoes and vegetables.

Lima Beans, Corn Beef
Chili and garlic adds to the vegetables and meat

INGREDIENTS

1	Can	Tomatoes
1/4	Cup	Beef stock
1		Carrot
1	Can	Lima beans
1		Onion
1	Clove	Garlic
		Salt and pepper to taste
1	Can	Corn beef
1	Crushed	Chili

DIRECTIONS

Mix the tomatoes with the beef stock. Add chopped carrots, onions, garlic, pepper, salt, and chili. Cook until the onion and carrot are tender and the sauce is just slightly thickened. Add drained can of lima beans and corn beef broken into chunks. Heat until the meat is hot, then serve.

If the gravy is not thick enough, mix a little cornstarch in cold water and add to the gravy when hot. Cook for an extra minute.

Shipboard Sausages
These sausages are made with canned meat

INGREDIENTS

1	Can	Corn beef
2	Cups	Dry bread crumbs
1	Tbl	Catsup
2		Eggs
1	Tbl	Worchestershire sauce
1	Clove	Garlic (optional)
		Salt and pepper to taste
2	Tbls	Water

DIRECTIONS

Mix the corn beef and bread crumbs thoroughly. Add the catsup, Worchestershire sauce, salt, and pepper. Mix in well-beaten eggs. Knead the mixture with your hands until well blended. Roll into sausage-size rolls. Roll the sausage in flour, then lightly in oil. Put into a hot skillet and shake-fry until they are golden brown all over. Add water to the pan, put the lid on, and let the sausage steam until cooked, about 15 minutes. More water may be necessary but only add a little at a time. Remove from the skillet and let cool on absorbent paper. Serve with catsup.

Use garlic, celery seed, nutmeg, cayenne pepper, finely minced onions, small whole peppercorns, or other spices to flavor the sausage. Mix any one of the above into the catsup before mixing with bread crumbs.

Party Patties of Luncheon Meat
Cloves give it a different flavor

INGREDIENTS

1	12-ounce	Can luncheon meat, ground
1/2	Cup	Soft bread crumbs
1/4	Cup	Catsup
1		Egg, slightly beaten
1/2	Tsp	Dry mustard
1/8	Tsp	Ground cloves
1	Medium	Onion, minced

DIRECTIONS

Mix all the above ingredients together and form into little round patties. Fry in butter, in a skillet with the lid on, for 5-7 minutes on one side. Turn over and fry on the other side until brown.

Tortillas from Mexico

INGREDIENTS

1	Cup	Flour
1/2	Cup	Cornmeal
1/4	Tsp	Salt
1		Egg
1 1/2	Cups	Cold water

DIRECTIONS

Combine the above ingredients in a bowl and beat until smooth. Spoon 3 tablesoons of batter onto a moderately hot, ungreased griddle. Tip the pan to spread the batter to make a 6-inch pancake. Turn the tortilla when the edges begin to look dry, not brown. Turn and bake the other side, again, not brown. Romove from pan and keep warm. Repeat until all the batter is used. Makes 12 tortillas.

Enchiladas from Mexico
Tortillas filled with corn beef and smothered in hot sauce

Filling:

INGREDIENTS

1	Can	Corn beef
1	Clove	Garlic, minced
		Dash tobasco
		Dash Worchestershire sauce
1		Onion, diced
2-3	Tbls	Enchilada sauce

DIRECTIONS

Mix the above ingredients together. Take a tortilla and put a couple of teaspoons of filling on one side. Roll up and set in a shallow dish. Continue until the dozen tortillas are rolled. Place 3-4 enchiladas on each plate. Pour heated sauce over them and serve immediately.

Sauce:

INGREDIENTS

1		Onion, diced
1	Clove	Garlic, minced
2	Small cans	Tomato puree
3-4	Tsps	Chili powder
1	Tsp	Salt
1/2	Tsp	Tobasco sauce
		Dash Worchestershire sauce

DIRECTIONS

Mix ingredients in a saucepan and simmer until thickened.

Skillet Pizza

INGREDIENTS

2	Cups	Flour
1/2	Tsp	Salt
1	Tsp	Baking powder
1		Egg, beaten
3	Tbls	Butter
		Milk

DIRECTIONS

Sift the flour, salt, and baking powder into a bowl. Cut the butter into the dry mixture. Add the beaen egg and enough milk to make a stiff dough. Lightly knead and roll into a circle ¼-inch thick. Fit inside the skillet.

Spread any of the following toppings on page 109 over the dough and cook over an asbestos pad on medium flame for approximately 15 minutes.

Frying Pan Pizza

INGREDIENTS

1 1/2	Cups	Flour
2	Tsps	Baking powder
4	Tbls	Butter or substitute
1/2	Tsp	Salt
1		Egg
1/3	Cup	Milk
		Sliced cheese

DIRECTIONS

Sift flour, baking powder, and salt into a bowl. Rub in the butter until the mixture looks like fine bread crumbs. Combine the egg and milk and add to the flour mixture. Mix until a soft dough. Roll the dough to the size required to cover a well-greased frying pan. Spread a topping over the dough and add sliced cheese. Cover with lid or aluminum foil and place frying pan on an asbestos pad over medium flame. Cook 12-15 minutes. Fill with any of the toppings on page 109.

Pizza Toppings

INGREDIENTS

1	Small can	Tomato paste
1	Medium	Onion, Chopped
1/2	Tsp	Sweet basil
1/2	Cup	Water
		Cheese slices

DIRECTIONS

Put all ingredients, except the cheese, into a saucepan, bring to a boil, and cook for 8-10 minutes. Let cool, spread over pizza dough, and top with cheese slices.

INGREDIENTS

1	Can	Tomato puree
1/2	Can	Water
1	Clove	Garlic, crushed
	Dash	Worchestershire sauce
		Sprinkle of basil
Scant	Tbl	Butter
		Salt and pepper to taste

DIRECTIONS

Slice onions into rings and put on dough. Add sliced mushrooms, green peppers, olives, and chopped tomatoes. Mix and heat the sauce ingredients and cook until thick. Spread sauce evenly on top of the vegetables.

(continued)

INGREDIENTS

1	Cup	Grated cheese
3-4		Tomatoes
1		Egg
1/4	Cup	Milk
1/4	Tsp	Grated nutmeg
6		Black olives

DIRECTIONS

Sprinkle grated cheese over the pastry. Add sliced tomatoes and chopped olives. Sprinkle with nutmeg. Mix the egg and milk together and pour over the pizza. Cook as recipe directs.

INGREDIENTS

1	Small can	Tomato puree
1	Can	Water
6	Tbls	Grated cheese
1	Tsp	Basil or oregano

DIRECTIONS

Pour the tomato puree and water over dough. Add herbs. Sprinkle with grated cheese. Cook pizza as directed.

VARIATIONS

Any of the following can be used with the sauces: crayfish, asparagus, corn beef chunks, sardines, salami, hard-boiled eggs, onion rings, shrimp, crisp fried bacon, anchovies, green peppers, bean sprouts, mushrooms, chopped parsley, tuna chunks, luncheon meat, chicken livers, and all types of cheese.

Sultana Fried Rice

Luncheon meat, sultanas, rice, and eggs

INGREDIENTS

2	Cups	Cooked rice
2	Tbls	Butter
1	Large	Onion
1/2	Cup	Luncheon meat, chopped
1	Tsp	Ginger
1/4	Cup	Sultanas or raisins
1	Large	Celery stalk or celery flakes
1	Tbl	Butter
2		Eggs
1	Cube	Chicken broth

DIRECTIONS

Melt the butter in a skillet. Add chopped onion and saute. Add sultanas, luncheon meat, and crumbled chicken broth cube. Mix and turn while cooking. Add salt and pepper to taste and ground ginger. Add cooked rice, fluffing with a fork. When heated, clear a corner in the skillet and add butter. When melted, add eggs. When eggs are cooked, blend into the rice mixture.

Curried Luncheon Meat
Apple and coconut in curry

INGREDIENTS

1	Can	Luncheon meat
2	Large	Onions
1	Tbl	Butter
1	Tbl	Curry
1	Tbl	Vinegar
1	Small can	Tomatoes
		Few raisins
1		Apple
1/4	Cup	Coconut
1	Small can	Evaporated milk
1	Cup	Water or beef broth
		Salt and pepper to taste

DIRECTIONS

Fry sliced onions in butter and add curry powder. Fry for a few seconds and then add the vinegar, tomatoes, and stock or water. Season with salt and pepper. Add the raisins and coconut. Cook for 30 minutes on low heat. Add milk, diced luncheon meat, and grated apple. Just heat and serve with rice.

Chili Beans
Easy with canned ingredients

INGREDIENTS

1	Can	Steak and onions
2	Cans	Red kidney beans
		Dash of tabasco sauce
		Salt and pepper
1	Tsp	Chili powder or 1 crushed chili
1	Small	Onion

(continued)

DIRECTIONS

Open the kidney beans and pour into a saucepan, juice and all. Add the tabasco, chili, diced onion, and salt and pepper to taste. Heat thoroughly and simmer for a few minutes. Stir so the beans do not stick to the bottom. Add the can of meat and heat until hot. Serve in soup bowls with crackers and butter.

You can make the chili beans early, let them set for a few hours, and then reheat before using. This marries the flavors.

Chili Corn Beef and Rice
Add more tabasco if you like it very hot

INGREDIENTS

2	Tbls	Butter
2	Cups	Cooked rice
1	Can	Tomatoes
1		Onion
1	Tsp	Salt
		Pepper to taste
1/4	Tsp	Tabasco sauce
1	Can	Corn beef

DIRECTIONS

Melt the butter in a skillet, add a diced onion, and saute a few minutes until the onion is transparent. Add the cooked rice. Mix well to coat the rice with butter. Add the tomatoes, salt, pepper, and tabasco. Mix well. Lastly add chunked corn beef. Discard any excess fat from the corn beef. Simmer for 5 minutes until piping hot.

Canned Ham Glazes
Transforms a canned ham into a glamorous party dish

DIRECTIONS

The following glazes are for 2 pound hams. Use half the recipe for smaller hams. Always remove any gelatine from the outside of the ham before heating it in a skillet over low heat.

Black Cherry Glaze

INGREDIENTS

1	Can	Black cherries
1	Tbl	Corn starch
2	Tbls	Port

DIRECTIONS

Drain the syrup of the cherries into a saucepan. Blend in the corn starch and add port. Stir over low heat until sauce thickens and boils. Decorate ham with cherries and pour glaze over them.

Brandy-Peach Glaze

INGREDIENTS

2	Tbls	Honey
1	Can	Sliced peaches
2	Tbls	Brandy
1/2	Tsp	Prepared mustard
		Ground cloves

DIRECTIONS

Combine the peach syrup, honey, brandy, and mustard in a saucepan. Heat until just boiling. Sprinkle cloves over hot ham, place it on a platter, and pour the glaze over it. Decorate with peach slices.

(continued)

Pineapple Glaze

INGREDIENTS

1	Can	Crushed pineapple
2	Tbls	Honey
1	Cup	Dry white wine
1	Tbl	Soy sauce
1	Tsp	Ground ginger
1	Small	Onion

DIRECTIONS

Combine the honey, wine, soy sauce, ginger, and chopped onion in a saucepan. Heat and add the crushed pineapple and syrup. Simmer for 5 minutes and then pour over heated ham.

Ham Fry

Sweet and sour sauce for canned ham

DIRECTIONS

Lightly fry ham slices on one side and gently turn over. Put slice of lemon on top and baste with the following sauce:

INGREDIENTS

1	Tbl	Corn syrup
1/2	Clove	Garlic crushed
		Salt and pepper to taste

DIRECTIONS

Mix the above and drizzle it over the ham while it is cooking. Serve hot with sweet potatoes.

Meat Dinners

Most of these dishes are one-pot meals.

A different herb or a drop of wine will add a delicate flavor to these simple dishes.

Beef Patties with Sage-Onion Potatoes
Seasoned potatoes between two patties of beef

INGREDIENTS

3		Onions
3	Tbls	Butter
5		Potatoes, cooked and diced
1 1/2	Tsps	Salt
1/2	Tsp	Pepper
1	Tsp	Ground sage
1/2	Tsp	Ground thyme
1	Lb	Minced beef

DIRECTIONS

Cook thinly sliced onions in butter until tender. Add potatoes, 1/2 teaspoon salt, 1/4 teaspoon pepper, sage, and thyme. Cook until the potatoes are browned. Stir occasionally to brown all over. Add the remaining salt and pepper to the minced beef and shape into 8 patties. Cook in the remaining butter to the desired doneness. Put the potatoes between two patties, sandwich fashion, and serve. Makes 4 servings.

Gingery Beef Pot Roast
Tangy hot flavor in tomato gravy

INGREDIENTS

3-4	Lbs	Beef
2	Tsps	Ginger
2	Tsps	Salt
1	Tsp	Tumeric
2		Onions, chopped
2	Cloves	Garlic, crushed
1	8-oz can	Tomatoes
1	Cup	Boullion Broth
1/2	Tsp	Dried red peppers

DIRECTIONS

Rub the meat with a mixture of ginger, tumeric, and salt. Heat enough oil in a heavy saucepan to brown the meat. When the meat is nicely browned on all sides, lift it out and put a rack in the saucepan. Replace the meat in a saucepan. Mix the rest of the ingredients and pour over the meat. Cover and simmer for 2 hours or until the meat is cooked. Place meat on a platter and make gravy out of the juices in the saucepan.

Chili Con Carne
Use canned beans or dried red beans

Dried Beans: Soak beans overnight in cold water, drain, put into saucepan, cover with fresh water, and cook for 2 hours until the beans are tender. Drain, but save 1 1/2 cups liquid.

Canned Beans: Reserve the liquid and make up to 1 1/2 cups with water.

INGREDIENTS

1	Large can	Beans in tomato sauce or
1	Cup	Dried red beans
2		Onions
1		Green pepper (optional)
2	Tbls	Oil
1 1/2	Cups	Liquid
1	Lb	Minced lean beef
1	Tsp	Salt
1/4	Tsp	Cumin
1-3	Tsps	Chili powder
1/2	Cup	Tomato puree (concentrated)
1	Clove	Garlic

DIRECTIONS

Chop the onion and green pepper and crush the garlic. Put oil in a large saucepan and saute the vegetables until golden brown. Stir in the meat and cook until colored. Use a fork to break up any chunks. Add salt, cumin, chili powder, and tomato puree. Add the liquid from beans. Mix well and heat to boiling. Add the beans, cover and cook for 30-40 minutes on low heat. Serve in bowls with buttered crackers.

Meat Loaf and Eggs
Bury the eggs in the meat mixture

INGREDIENTS

1/4	Lb	Bacon
1	Lb	Sausage meat
1/2	Lb	Minced meat
1/2	Cup	Fine bread crumbs
1	Tbl	Parsley
1		Beaten egg
		Salt and pepper to taste
2		Hard-boiled eggs

DIRECTIONS

Chop bacon finely. Mix the bacon, minced meat, sausage meat, bread crumbs, parsley, salt, and pepper and egg together. Grease a pudding bowl and press half the meat mixture into it. Make two slight indentations and press the hard-boiled eggs into them. Press the rest of the meat mixture around the eggs and level off the top. Tie foil or greaseproof paper over the top. Steam for 2 hours in a deep saucepan partially filled with water. Don't let the pan boil dry. When cold, turn the meat loaf onto a platter. Garnish with parsley.

Quick Moussaka from Greece
An easy top-of-the-stove method

INGREDIENTS

1	Lb	Minced beef or lamb
1		Onion
		Salt and pepper
1	Medium	Eggplant
		Mashed potatoes for 4
2	Tbls	Butter
2	Tbls	Flour
1 1/2	Cups	Milk
1/2	Cup	Cheese
		Bread crumbs

DIRECTIONS

Peel the eggplant and cut into thin slices. Saute in oil in a frying pan and cook until tender. Remove and set aside.

Saute chopped onion in a skillet, add minced beef, salt, and pepper. Stir fry until meat is cooked. Set aside.

Slowly melt butter in a saucepan. Remove from heat and add flour. Gradually stir in milk. Bring to a boil and add salt, pepper, and grated cheese.

Place a layer of potatoes in a casserole dish. top with a layer of meat, then a layer of eggplant, and so on until all mixtures are used. Top with the cheese sauce. Sprinkle on browned bread crumbs.

Note: Just before layering into casserole dish, reheat each of the mixtures. This dish can be made ahead of time and reheated at the last minute before layering into casserole.

Smyrna Sausages from Greece
Made with chopped meat and bread crumbs

INGREDIENTS

1 1/2	Lbs	Minced lean meat
1	Cup	Moist bread crumbs
3	Cloves	Garlic, crushed
1		Onion, chopped finely
1	Tsp	Cumin seeds
1	Can	Tomatoes
1	Tsp	Sugar
		Salt and pepper

DIRECTIONS

Mix the meat, bread crumbs, garlic, onion, cumin seeds, salt, and pepper.
Make into rolls and shape like sausages. Fry in hot oil until cooked and
browned.

Mix the tomatoes, sugar, salt, and pepper in a saucepan and simmer for
15 minutes. Add the sausages and just heat. Serve.

DIRECTIONS
Meat Loaf, Pot Roast Style
Tomato juice, sage, and onions mixed with beef

INGREDIENTS

1/2	Cup	Tomato juice
1/2	Cup	Dry bread crumbs
1	Lb	Minced beef
		Salt and pepper to taste
1		Egg
1/2	Tsp	Dried sage
1		Onion
1/2	Cup	Water
3	Tbls	Vegetable oil

Mix the bread crumbs with the tomato juice and add the rest of the seasoning, finely chopped onion, minced beef, and egg. Knead well and form into a round that will fit a heavy saucepan.

Put oil in a saucepan and heat until very hot. Put the meat loaf into the hot oil and brown it. Put the asbestos pad on top of the flame and set the saucepan on it. When the asbestos pad is hot, turn the flame down and let meat loaf cook for 45 minutes on very low heat. You can make a log-shaped loaf that will turn over in the saucepan if you want to brown all sides. Cook for same length of time.

Stifado

It's the sweetness of the onions that makes this Greek dish so delicious

INGREDIENTS

1	Lb	Lean beef cut into chunks the size of half an egg
2	Lbs	Small onions
2	Large	Tomatoes, peeled, seeded and cut into small pieces
3		Bay leaves
		Salt and pepper to taste
2	Tbls	Vinegar

DIRECTIONS

Use half butter and half oil to brown the meat in a deep heavy saucepan. Add the tomatoes, bay leaves, salt, pepper, and vinegar. Simmer for a few minutes to mix the flavors. Add peeled, whole onions, and just enough water to half cover the contents of the saucepan. Cover with a lid and simmer until meat is tender and the liquid is reduced to gravy. Serve with boiled potatoes.

Roast Beef with Baked Potatoes
All cooked on top of the stove

DIRECTIONS

Cut the beef into 2-inch cubes. Crush 1 clove of garlic into 1/2 teaspoon salt. Pour enough oil into the saucepan to just cover the bottom. Heat until the oil is smoky hot. Stir the garlic-salt into the hot oil. Add the meat chunks and brown on all sides. Only brown a few at a time. Remove the meat and set on a platter.

Peel potatoes about the same size as the meat. Add more oil to the pan and let it get very hot. Toss the potatoes in the oil and let them brown. Pour out most of the excess oil.

Put the meat back in the saucepan. Put the asbestos pad under the saucepan and leave the flame high. Cook the potatoes and meat for about 10 minutes, shaking the pan occasionally to turn the meat and potatoes. Turn flame down, put lid on, and cook for another 5-10 minutes until potatoes are tender. With a little practice you will have browned potatoes and meat that will look as though they came out of the oven.

VARIATIONS

Serve yam puffs (see recipe, page 183) with meat instead of potatoes.

Use pork instead of beef.

Short Ribs of Beef
Simmer in a skillet

INGREDIENTS

2	Lbs	Beef short ribs cut into 2-inch pieces
		Salt and pepper to taste

DIRECTIONS

Dredge the short ribs in flour and season with salt and pepper. Brown them in oil in a heavy skillet. When browned, drain off the excess oil. Cover the ribs, about 3/4 the way up with water. Put lid on skillet and simmer for 2 hours. Turn the meat several times to prevent it from sticking to the pan. Add more water if necessary. When the meat is tender, let the liquid thicken to gravy. Serve with mashed potatoes.

VARIATIONS

Add onions chopped fine, dash of Worchestershire sauce, or dash chili sauce, or use tomato juice instead of water.

Porcupine Meat Balls
Rice, meat, and tomato sauce

INGREDIENTS

1	Lb	Ground meat
1		Onion, chopped fine
1/2	Cup	Raw rice
		Salt and pepper to taste
1/8	Tsp	Sweet basil
1	Can	Tomato soup
1/2	Can	Water

DIRECTIONS

Mix the first four ingredients together and form into little round balls. Arrange them on a trivet in a heavy saucepan. Mix water with the soup, add sweet basil, salt, and pepper, and pour over the meat balls. Heat on top of the stove until the soup boils. Turn the burner down and simmer until the rice is cooked. Gently lift the meat balls out of the saucepan onto a platter and thicken the tomato gravy, if necessary, before serving.

Oriental Meat Balls
Sweet and sour sauce with fresh or canned meat

INGREDIENTS

1	Lb	Minced meat or
1	Can	Meat minced
1 1/2	Cups	Bread crumbs
1		Egg
		Salt
2	Tbls	Worchestershire sauce
1/2	Cup	Milk (less if using canned meat)

DIRECTIONS

Mix the above ingredients and form into 1-inch balls. Shake-fry in a skillet with oil until browned. Remove from skillet and put in serving dish. Pour the following sauce over the meat balls.

Sauce

INGREDIENTS

1/4	Cup	Marmalade
3	Tbls	Soy sauce
2	Tbls	Lemon juice
1/4	Cup	Peanut butter
3-4	Tbls	Water

DIRECTIONS

Mix the above ingredients in a saucepan and heat. Stir until the sauce is smooth and hot. Pour over the meat balls. Serve with rice.

"Honnalee's" Stew

An easy to prepare stew with many variations

INGREDIENTS

1-2	Lbs	Beef
2	Cloves	Crushed garlic
3-4		Onions, halved
2	Medium	Potatoes, sliced
3		Carrots sliced lengthwise
1/2	Cup	Macaroni
1	Can	Peeled tomatoes
	Dash	tabasco (optional)
		Salt and pepper to taste
1	Tsp	(Heaping) Beef extract or
2		Beef cubes
1/2	Cup	Wine
1/2	Cup	Water

DIRECTIONS

Brown small pieces of beef in a little oil in the bottom of a heavy saucepan. Add the other ingredients. Put on the lid and cook gently until the potatoes, carrots, and macaroni are tender. The liquid should be reduced to gravy. If the liquid is too thin, add a little corn starch mixed with water to thicken.

VARIATIONS

When potatoes are half cooked, add the flowerettes from 1/2 small cauliflower.

Add freeze dry peas or beans when the potatoes are partially cooked. If using canned peas, drain and add just before serving.

Add sliced green peppers or mushrooms when potatoes are nearly cooked.

Rissoles with Hot Chili Sauce
Little meat rolls with chili and wine sauce

INGREDIENTS

1	Lb	Minced beef
1	Lb	Sausage meat
1/2	Cup	Chopped parsley
1	Small	Onion, grated
2	Tsp	Salt
		Pepper to taste
1	Cup	Bread crumbs
2		Eggs

DIRECTIONS

Combine the above ingredients with your hands and form into little rolls. Roll them in fine bread crumbs and fry in hot cooking oil until brown. Drain on paper. Pour excess oil from the pan and make sauce.

Sauce

INGREDIENTS

1/2	Cup	Red wine
1/2	Tsp	Cumin
1	Tsp	Chili powder
1	Clove	Garlic, crushed

DIRECTIONS

Add wine to the pan and scrape off any brown bits. Add the remaining ingredients and mix well. Allow to simmer for a few minutes. Pour over the rissoles and serve.

Pigs in a Blanket
Cabbage leaves stuffed with pork and rice

INGREDIENTS

3/4	Lb	Lean pork, minced
1/2	Cup	Uncooked rice
1 1/2	Tsps	Salt
1/4	Tsp	Pepper
8		Cabbage leaves
1	Small	Onion, minced
1	Can	Tomato soup or
1	Large can	Tomato juice
3/4	Cup	Water for soup

DIRECTIONS

Mix the minced pork, rice, salt, pepper, and onion. Cook the cabbage
leaves in boiling salted water until just limp. Drain and let cabbage leaves
cool. Fill each leaf with the meat mixture and roll up. Place the rolls on a
trivet in the bottom of a saucepan. Mix the soup with water, season to
taste, and pour over the cabbage rolls. If using tomato juice, use just
enough to cover the cabbage rolls. Put lid on saucepan and cook on top
of stove for 30 minutes. Carefully lift the rolls out and place on platter.
Thicken the tomato sauce and pour over the cabbage rolls.

VARIATIONS

Use minced beef instead of pork.

Use a mixture of beef and pork.

Use oregano in the meat mixture for a different flavor.

Pork Chop Casserole
One pot meal with mushroom sauce

INGREDIENTS

2-6	Medium	Pork chops
1-2	Medium	Onions
		Potatoes
		Salt and pepper
1	Can	Mushroom soup
1	Can	Water

DIRECTIONS

Fry pork chops until brown on both sides. Arrange them in the bottom of a large saucepan. Saute chopped onions in the pork fat and brownings. Add 1 can water and 1 can mushroom soup. Mix well. Peel the potatoes and slice over the pork chops. Pour the liquid mushroom mixture over the potatoes. Simmer until the potatoes are cooked. Serve hot.

Pork in Wine and Mushroom Sauce
Use mushroom soup, onions, and wine

INGREDIENTS

1		Pork shoulder chop for each person
1	Can	Mushroom soup
4		Onions, peeled and quartered
		Good sprinkling of oregano
		Salt and pepper to taste
1/2	Cup	Wine, red or white
1/2	Cup	Water

DIRECTIONS

Brown each pork chop in a little oil in a skillet. Move each chop when browned into a saucepan and put a layer of onions and a sprinkling of oregano between each layer of chops. When chops are all browned, add wine to skillet to get all the good brown bits out of it. Add water and mushroom soup. Mix well and season to taste. Pour the mixture over the pork chops. Cover with the lid and simmer for 30 minutes, until chops are tender and the liquid is reduced to thick gravy. If necessary to reduce the gravy more, remove the lid and cook until the gravy is the right consistency. Serve with potatoes and vegetables.

Shish Kebab
Top of the stove method

DIRECTIONS

Place the meat and vegetables on skewers that will fit a skillet. Marinate for 15 minutes, turning often, in one of the following marinades. Lay the skewered meat in hot skillet. Put lid on and shake-fry until meat is cooked. Do a few at a time. When all shish kebabs are cooked, serve them with rissoto or pilaf (see page 176).

Marinades

1 part lemon juice, 3 parts olive oil, and oregano seasoning.

1 mashed garlic clove, 3/4 cup sweet sherry, and 1/2 cup soy sauce.

Veal Rolls
Veal stuffed with bacon cooked in wine

INGREDIENTS

4	Slices	Veal, thin
4	Slices	Bacon
2	Tbls	Seasoned flour
1/2	Cup	Red wine
1	Cup	Water
1	Clove	Garlic
1		Onion, chopped
1/4	Cup	Mushrooms
		Salt and pepper to taste

DIRECTIONS

Cut the sliced veal in 2x4-inch strips. Cut bacon in half. Put half a slice of bacon in the center of each piece of veal. Roll up and secure with a toothpick. Roll in seasoned flour. Heat enough oil in a heavy skillet to brown the meat rolls and add a crushed garlic clove as the oil heats. Brown the rolls on all sides. Pour off any excess oil. Add red wine and water. Cover skillet with lid and simmer for 20 minutes. Add more water if necessary. Remove lid and add the chopped onion and mushrooms. Simmer for 10 minutes more until the liquid has a gravy-like consistency. Serve with mashed potatoes and green peas.

VARIATIONS

Use thin slices of beef instead of veal. Use oregano, basil, or thyme for seasoning.

Calves Liver in Wine

INGREDIENTS

2	Lbs	Calf liver
2	Tbls	Butter
		Flour
		Salt and pepper
4		Tomatoes, peeled and quartered
1	Cup	Red wine
3/4	Cup	Smoked bacon, chopped
1	Cup	Onions, chopped
1	Cup	Carrots, chopped

DIRECTIONS

Clean and slice the liver and drench in seasoned flour. Fry the bacon bits in a skillet and when crisp, remove. Fry the liver until browned on both sides. Remove the liver and add the wine to the brownings. Stir until well mixed. Place the liver back in the skillet. Put in onions, carrots, and tomatoes in layers with bacon on top. Cover with lid and cook over low heat for 20 minutes or until the vegetables are tender. It may be necessary to add a little water. The liver should be surrounded by rich gravy. Serve with mashed potatoes.

Kidney Sauce
Over vegetables or spaghetti

INGREDIENTS

8		Lamb kidneys
2		Onions
1	Clove	Garlic
3		Tomatoes, skinned and chopped
1	Tbl	Lard
1	Tbl	Flour
		Salt and pepper to taste
1		Beef cube
1/2	Cup	Hot water
2	Tbls	Tomato puree
4	Tbls	Red wine
1		Bay leaf
1/2	Tsp	Oregano or thyme

DIRECTIONS

Wash and dry the kidneys. Remove skins and snip away cores. Chop roughly. Melt lard in a saucepan. Add diced onions and saute until golden brown. Add the crushed garlic and kidneys and stir fry for 5 minutes. Add the flour and cook gently for another 2 minutes. Remove from the heat and stir in the stock. Add the rest of the ingredients and bring to a boil. Turn the flame down and simmer for 25-30 minutes until the sauce thickens. Discard the bay leaf. Serve over vegetables or spaghetti.

Kidneys in Wine
Serve on hot toast

INGREDIENTS

4		Lamb kidneys
2	Tbls	Butter or substitute
1		Onion
2	Tbls	Chopped parsley
		Salt and pepper
1/4	Lb	Mushrooms or
1	Small can	Mushrooms
1	Tbl	Flour
4	Tbls	Port wine

DIRECTIONS

Skin the kidneys. Cut them in half and remove the center cores. Soak in salted water for 15 minutes. Drain and dry. Peel and chop onion. Melt butter in pan and add onion and kidneys. Saute for 5 minutes. Add sliced mushrooms, salt, and pepper. Cook 5 more minutes. Mix the port wine and flour together, add to the kidneys, and stir until the mixture boils and thickens. Stir in parsley. Place on hot buttered toast. Serves two.

Fish Dishes

Fish is delicate, so treat it with care. Different kinds of fish have distinctive flavors and textures. These characteristics damage easily with overcooking.

Cook fish gently until the flesh flakes easily when tested with a fork. Never overcook fish or let it dry.

Fresh or canned fish can be used for numerous dishes because fish combines wonderfully with many spices, seasonings, and sauces.

Fish served with parsley-buttered potatoes, fresh bread and butter, and a good white wine is the ultimate.

Baked Fish in Foil

DIRECTIONS

Clean and scale the fish. Rub it with a little salt. Sprinkle on lemon juice and dot with butter. Wrap in a double layer of foil after it has been cut into pieces that will fit into a skillet. Put another double layer of foil on the bottom of the skillet. Put the wrapped fish on top. Cover with lid and cook over medium heat until fish flakes easily. The time depends on the thickness of the fish.

Creamed Fish Rissoles
Delicious, crisp rissoles

DIRECTIONS

Make a very stiff white sauce (see recipe on page 161). Season well with salt and pepper. Add flaked cooked fish to the hot sauce. Pour into a flat dish and let set. When set, take spoonfuls and drop into a beaten egg and then roll in bread crumbs. Fry in hot oil. Drain on absorbent paper and serve hot.

Curry Fish Balls
Curried fish, rice, and coconut sauce

INGREDIENTS

1	Can	Tuna fish
1	Medium	onion
1	Tbl	Flour
		Salt and pepper
2	Tbls	Cooking oil
1	Tbl	Curry powder
3	Tbls	Desiccated coconut

DIRECTIONS

Drain the oil from the tuna. Add chopped onion, flour, salt, and pepper to the tuna meat. Mix well and form into balls. Heat oil in a skillet and gently fry the fish balls, turning them until they are golden brown. Shaking the skillet will also turn the fish balls. When they are golden all over, sprinkle with curry powder and shake the skillet back and forth to coat them with the powder. Serve with hot rice and coconut sauce.

Coconut sauce

Make a cup of thin white sauce (see page 161) and add desiccated coconut. Cook for 2-3 minutes. Strain if you don't like the coconut fiber in the sauce. Add to the brownings in the skillet. Stir well; then pour the sauce over the fish balls.

Fish Loaf
Pressure cooked

INGREDIENTS

1	Lb	Fish
2	Tbls	Butter
1/4	Cup	Bread crumbs
		Parsley
1/2	Cup	Milk
2		Eggs
1/2	Tsp	Anchovie sauce
		Cayenne pepper

(continued)

DIRECTIONS

Separate the eggs and beat the whites stiff. Set aside to add to the mixture later. Combine fish, butter, bread crumbs, milk, egg yolks, anchovie sauce, and dash cayenne pepper. Mix well and add the chopped parsley.

Fold in the beaten egg whites. Put the mixture into a greased bowl and cover it with several layers of greased paper and one thickness of foil.

Put rack into a pressure cooker and add 1/2 cup of water. Set bowl on rack and put on lid. Bring up to 15 pounds pressure and cook for 12-15 minutes. Cool the cooker and remove the bowl. Turn upside down and ease out the fish loaf. Serve in slices with mashed potatoes and green beans.

French Style Braised Fish
The fish is cooked on a layer of vegetables

INGREDIENTS

Cut into thin strips: 3 carrots, 3 onions, 1 clove of garlic, and 2 stalks of celery. Saute in 3 tablespoons butter for 4-5 minutes. Add salt and peppe (optional; add chopped parsley or 1 teaspoon thyme). Arrange the vegetables in the bottom of a skillet or saucepan.

Place the fish, which has been cleaned and scaled, on top of the bed of vegetables. Salt and pepper the fish and lay a couple of strips of bacon or salt pork on top of it. Add enough wine, red or white, or mix wine with equal amounts of fish bouillon, to cover the vegetables.

Cover with lid and cook slowly over asbestos pad. Baste fish with the wine liquid often, until it is cooked. Place the fish on a platter and decorate with lemon slices.

VARIATION

Mash the vegetables and juice through a sieve, reheat, and pour over the fish.

Herring in Tomato Sauce on Rice
Easy, quick, and different using canned herring

INGREDIENTS

1	Tbl	Butter
1	Tsp	Indian hot curry powder (heaping)
1	Can	Herring in tomato sauce
1		Onion chopped fine

DIRECTIONS

Saute the onion in butter. Chop the herrings into chunks and add with the tomato sauce to the onions. Sprinkle with the curry powder and heat until hot. Serve over hot rice.

Kedgeree
Use cooked or canned fish

INGREDIENTS

1	Cup	Cooked rice
		Cold boiled fish or can of salmon or tuna
4		Hard boiled eggs
		Salt and pepper
		Thyme
2	Tbls	Butter (approx.)

DIRECTIONS

Mix the boiled rice and cold fish together. Put butter in a saucepan large enough to hold the mixture. Melt the butter and add the seasoning. Add the rice-fish mixture and stir well until heated through. Chop the eggs fine and add to the mixture. Serve while hot.

VARIATIONS

Add a pinch of curry powder. Add chopped parsley instead of thyme. Chop 1 onion fine and add to fish.

Kedgeree Special
Use a can of smoked fish fillets

INGREDIENTS

2	Tbls	Butter
1		Onion
1	Small	Cooking apple
2	Tsp	Curry powder
1	Tsp	Salt
		Pepper to taste
11-oz.	Can	Smoked fish fillets
2	Cups	Cooked rice
2		Hard-boiled eggs
		Chopped parsley

DIRECTIONS

Heat the butter in a pan and saute the finely chopped onion, and apple. When they are tender, stir in the curry powder, salt, and pepper.

Break up the fish fillets, discarding the bones and skin. Stir the fish and rice into the onion mixture and continue to stir until it is well blended and heated through. Just before serving, add the finely chopped eggs. Place the mixture on a serving plate and sprinkle with chopped parsley.

Kofta Ka Kari
East Indian curry over rice

INGREDIENTS

1	6-ounce	Can flaked tuna
1	Tbl	Grated onion
1/8	Tsp	Ground ginger
1/8	Tsp	Garlic powder
3	Tbls	Dry bread crumbs
1		Egg, beaten
3-4		Green onions, sliced
1	Cup	Diced, peeled cucmber
1/2	Cup	Diced green pepper
2	Cups	Chicken broth
1	Tsp	Curry powder
2	Tbls	Soft butter
2	Tbls	Flour
2	Tbls	Oil

DIRECTIONS

Mix the undrained tuna with onion, ginger, garlic powder, bread crumbs, and egg. Season with salt and pepper and form into 1-inch balls. Saute in hot oil until browned, shaking the pan occasionally.

Lift out fish balls and add the green onion, cucumber, and green pepper. Stir fry 2-3 minutes. Add chicken broth and bring to a boil. Stir curry powder, butter, and flour into a smooth paste. Whisk it into the liquid and cook until thickened. Add the fish balls. Cover and simmer for 10 minutes. Mound the rice in the middle of a plate. Arrange fish balls around the outside. Pour the sauce over the fish balls and rice.

Solomon Islands Fish Cakes
Use any kind of sea food, including octopus

INGREDIENTS

1/2	Cup	Chopped onion
1/2	Tsp	Salt
1 1/2	Cups	Boiled fish
1 1/2	Cups	Cooked rice
1/2	Cup	Flour
2	Tbls	Worchestershire or soy sauce

DIRECTIONS

Mix all the above ingredients together. Form into thick patties. Cook in
deep fat or oil or fry in a skillet. When brown on one side, turn over and
cook until the other side is brown. Serve with sliced lemon.

Salt Cod Supreme
Salt cod with chick peas and boiled potatoes

INGREDIENTS

1	Lb	Salt cod
2	Tbls	Butter
2	Cups	Milk
2	Tbls	Flour
		Salt and white pepper
		Fresh or dried parsley
1	Can	Chick peas

DIRECTIONS

Cover salt cod with fresh water and soak for 24 hours.(You can also soak the cod in sea water and change the water three or four times before finally soaking it in fresh water.) Drain and cut into 1-inch chunks, cover with fresh cold water, bring to a boil, and simmer for 30 minutes.

Melt butter or substitute in a saucepan. Add one cup of milk and heat almost to boiling. Mix flour with a cup of milk until smooth. Remove the saucepan from the stove and stir in the flour-milk mixture. Return pan to the stove and cook over low flame. Stir constantly to avoid lumps while the sauce thickens; add more milk if sauce is too thick. Add salt and white pepper to taste and throw in lots of chopped fresh parsley or dried parsley flakes.

Heat 1-pound can of chick peas in their juice, drain, and mix with the cod. Pour the sauce over both peas and cod and serve with boiled potatoes.

Easy Canned Salmon Dinner

INGREDIENTS

1	8-oz can	Salmon
1	Can	Mushroom soup
1/2	Can	Mixed vegetables
1	Large	Onion
1	Tbl	Butter
1/2	Cup	Raw rice

(continued)

DIRECTIONS

Fry a diced onion in butter, add the rice, and stir fry. When the rice is coated and turns opaque, add a can of mushroom soup, the juice from the salmon, and just enough water to cover the rice. Boil for a few minutes; then turn the heat down and simmer until the rice is tender. Add the drained vegetables and salmon, from which the bones and skin have been removed. Reheat and serve.

Salmon Loaf

INGREDIENTS

2/3	Cup	Bread crumbs
2/3	Cup	Milk
1	8-oz can	Salmon
3/4	Cup	Mayonnaise or yogurt
2	Tbls	Lemon juice
1/3	Cup	Chopped onions
2	Tbls	Chopped parsley
2		Eggs, well-beaten
1/2	Tsp	Salt

DIRECTIONS

Soak bread crumbs in the milk for 10 minutes. Mix the balance of the ingredients and add them to the bread crumbs. Mix well and pour into a buttered pudding dish. Cover with foil. Steam for 1 hour in deep saucepan partially filled with water.

146

Salmon in Toasted Almond Sauce

INGREDIENTS

1	16 oz can	Salmon
1/2	Cup	Chopped almonds
1/4	Cup	Butter
1/4	Cup	Flour
1/2	Tsp	Salt
3	Cups	Cooked rice
2	Cups	Liquid (salmon juice and milk)
1	5 oz can	Mushrooms

DIRECTIONS

Drain the salmon and save the liquid. Break salmon into chunks and crush bones. Cook almonds in butter until golden brown. Blend in the flour and salt. Add the liquid gradually. Cook and stir until thickened. Add salmon chunks and mushrooms. Simmer for a few minutes. Serve over hot rice.

Scalloped Tuna

Canned tuna, bread crumbs, and spices

INGREDIENTS

1	7 oz can	Tuna chunks
3/4	Cup	Coarse cracker crumbs
1/2	Cup	Chopped parsley
1/2	Cup	Chopped celery
1	Clove	Garlic, crushed
1	Large	Onion, chopped
		Salt and pepper
1/2		Green pepper, seeded and chopped
1/4	Cup	Melted butter
1		Slightly beaten egg

(continued)

DIRECTIONS

Mix the cracker crumbs, tuna chunks, chopped vegetables, and seasoning together. Pour melted butter over them and mix until well combined. Slowly mix in the beaten egg. Put into a well-oiled frying pan, cover with lid, and cook over asbestos pad for about 20 minutes or until top is cooked. Turn onto a platter so brown side shows. Garnish with parsley and serve with peas and potatoes.

Tuna Rice Fritters

Fritters cooked in deep hot oil

INGREDIENTS

2	Cups	Cooked rice
1	Large can	Tuna fish
		Salt and pepper to taste
1/4	Cup	Milk
2	Tbls	Flour
2		Eggs

DIRECTIONS

Mix the rice, tuna, milk, and flour together. Add the eggs and mix well. Add seasoning to taste. Drop by spoonfuls into hot oil and cook until golden brown. Serve for lunch with a salad.

VARIATIONS

Add grated lemon peel to rice mixture.

Use any type of canned or fresh fish.

Use cinnamon, curry, or a little nutmeg to season.

Clam Fritters

Use fresh or canned clams

INGREDIENTS

2		Eggs
1/2	Cup	Milk
1/2	Cup	Clam juice
3/4	Cup	Flour
1	Tsp	Baking powder
1	Cup	Minced clams
		Salt and pepper

DIRECTIONS

Mix all the above ingredients to a smooth batter. Drop by teaspoonfuls into a hot buttered skillet. Cook until golden brown, approximately 5 minutes. Turn once only and cook until brown. Serve with lemon juice or lemon wedges.

Clam Patties

Use cooked mashed potatoes

INGREDIENTS

1	Can	Minced clams
1	Cup	Cooked mashed potatoes
2	Tbls	Butter
1/4	Tsp	Salt
1/8	Tsp	Nutmeg
1/2	Tbl	Lemon juice
1		Egg slightly beaten

DIRECTIONS

Drain the minced clams and combine with the mashed potatoes, butter, salt, nutmeg, and lemon juice. Add the beaten egg and mix well. Shape into 6 patties and deep fry in hot fat until lightly browned on both sides or fry in butter in a skillet. Serve with vegetables and lemon slices.

Potato Clam Fritters

INGREDIENTS

3	Large	Potatoes
3		Well-beaten eggs
1		Onion, chopped fine
1/2	Tsp	Salt
		Pepper to taste
4-6	Tbls	Flour
2	Cups	Finely minced clams or
1	Large can	Clams drained

DIRECTIONS

Peel and grate the potatoes and let soak overnight or for at least 3-4 hours. Drain off the excess liquid. Add the rest of the above ingredients, using enough flour to make a stiff batter that will form into patties. Fry the patties in butter until golden brown; turn and brown the other side. Serve with lemon wedges and salad.

Spaghetti and Mussel Sauce

INGREDIENTS

1	Qt.	Mussels
1	Small	Onion
1	Can	Tomato puree and enough liquid to make 2 Cups
1	Clove	Garlic, crushed
		Salt and pepper
1	Tbl	Chopped parsley
2	Tbls	Grated cheese

DIRECTIONS

Wash the mussels well, place in a large pan, and cover with water. Peel the onion and add to the water. Simmer for 5 minutes.

Remove mussels from their shells and discard the outer ring. Heat tomato puree, water (use the liquid from the mussels instead of fresh water), salt, pepper, and garlic. Simmer until sauce thickens. Add the mussels. Pour over cooked spaghetti and serve with grated cheese.

Spaghetti and Clam Sauce

INGREDIENTS

1	Cup	Chopped onion
4-5	Cloves	Garlic, crushed
1/2	Cup	Chopped parsley
1/2	Cup	Butter
1	Tsp	Salt
		Pepper to taste
1	Tsp	Dried basil
1	16-oz	Can clams

DIRECTIONS

Drain the clams and save the liquid. Add water to the liquid to make 2 cups. Saute the onion in butter until almost tender. Add parsley, clams, clam juice, salt, pepper, and basil and bring to a boil. Boil for 5 minutes until the flavors are well-blended. If the sauce is too thin, add a little corn starch mixed with water to the hot sauce to thicken it. Serve over hot spaghetti that has been cooked according to package directions.

Five Sauces in Which to Pan Fry Oysters
Serve hot on buttered toast

DIRECTIONS

Drain off the liquid and dry the oysters on absorbent paper.

1. Melt butter. Add lime juice, salt, pepper and a dash of cayenne pepper. When hot, add the oysters and heat until oysters are hot.

2. Melt butter and add a dash of Worchestershire sauce and 2 tablespoons catsup. When hot, add the drained oysters.

3. Melt butter. Add finely chopped onion. Saute for a few minutes. Add a dash of red wine and the drained oysters.

4. Melt butter. Add crushed garlic, 3 tablespoons tomato puree, dash white wine, and lemon juice. Heat and add oysters.

5. Fry bacon until crisp. Crumble, add chopped green onion, and 1/4 cup bread crumbs, and just brown. Add oysters. If necessary, add a small amount of oyster juice. Serve on buttered toast when hot with fried eggs or plain.

Fried Oysters
Fresh or canned oysters

INGREDIENTS

1	Can	Oysters
2	Tsps	Baking powder
1	Cup	Flour
1/4	Tsp	Salt
1	Tsp	Sugar

DIRECTIONS

Drain the oysters and save the liquid. Set the oysters on absorbent
paper to dry. Sift the flour, baking powder, and salt together into a bowl.
Add sugar and mix well. Add the oyster juice, and if necessary, enough
water to make a medium thick batter. Dip the oysters into the batter
and fry them until golden brown. Drain on paper. Serve on buttered
toast with slices of lemon.

The oysters can also be fried in butter after being dipped in the batter.
Turn them over when one side is golden brown and brown the other side.

Easy Oyster Pie
Made in a skillet with canned oysters

INGREDIENTS

1	Can	Oysters
2		Eggs
1	Tsp	Baking powder
		Salt and pepper to taste
1/2	Cup	Flour (approx.)
1	Tbl	Margarine

DIRECTIONS

Drain the oysters but save the juice. Sift the flour in a bowl and add baking powder, salt, and pepper. Make a fairly stiff batter using the juice plus a little water. Add the eggs, one at a time, beating well between each addition. Add a little more water to make a pancake-consistency batter. Melt butter in a skillet and pour in the batter. Arrange the oysters in the batter so they are evenly distributed. Put the lid on the skillet and turn the heat down. Cook over asbestos pad until the mixture is done. Cut into wedges and serve with lemon.

Hangtown Fry

INGREDIENTS

3		Eggs
1	Can	Oysters
2	Tbls	Butter
		Salt and peper to taste
1	Tbl	Cream or evaporated milk

DIRECTIONS

Beat the eggs with the cream until fluffy. Add the seasoning. Drain the oysters. Melt the butter in a skillet and add the oysters. Cook until slightly browned. Then pour the egg mixture over the oysters. Put a lid on the skillet and cook on low flame until the eggs are set. Serve with salad or on hot buttered toast.

Sauces

It's the sauce that makes a gourmet smile, for a sauce enhances what otherwise might be plain fair.

A La King Sauce
Make leftovers into a gourmet meal

INGREDIENTS

3	Tbls	Butter
3	Tbls	Flour
1/2	Tsp	Salt
		Dash pepper
1 1/2	Cups	Milk
1		Egg yolk
		Dash dry sherry
		Mushroms, green peppers, onions,
		or whatever, chopped

DIRECTIONS

Saute onions and vegetables in butter. Add flour, salt, and pepper. Mix well into the butter and gradually add milk. Stir constantly as the sauce thickens. Add a beaten egg yolk and a dash of sherry. When sauce thickens, add the leftovers, e.g., chicken, veal, sliced hard-boiled eggs, flaked fish, canned fish, beef, or whatever. Serve on hot buttered toast.

Uncooked Mustard Sauce
Serve with fish and rice

INGREDIENTS

2		Egg yolks
1	Tbl	Dry mustard
1/2	Tsp	Sugar
1/2	Tsp	Salt
1	Cup	Olive oil
2	Tbls	Vinegar
2	Tbls	Fresh parsley

DIRECTIONS

Beat the egg yolks and add mustard, sugar, and salt. Mix well and add
the olive oil, a drop at a time, beating constantly until the sauce thickens.
Add vinegar and chopped parsley and beat well. Serve with fish and rice.

Rough Weather Sauce
Easy to make and has a curry flavor

INGREDIENTS

1/2	Cup	Tomato juice
1/4	Cup	Chopped onions
1		Tomato, chopped
2	Sprigs	Parsley, chopped
1/2	Tsp	Chili
2	Tsps	Corn starch
1/4	Cup	Water
		Salt and pepper
1	Tsp	Hot curry powder

DIRECTIONS

Put tomato juice into a saucepan and bring to a boil. Add tomato, onion,
parsley, chili, salt, and pepper and boil for 2 minutes. Mix the corn starch
with water and add to the tomato mixture. Stir constantly until sauce
thickens. Add the curry powder and simmer for a few more minutes.
Remove from heat and let sit for 10-15 minutes to marry the flavors.
Reheat and serve over rice with meat.

Peanut Butter Sauce

INGREDIENTS

1/2	Cup	Water
1/4	Cup	Peanut butter
1	Tbl	Ground hot pepper or
2		Mashed chili peppers
1	Tbl	Soy sauce
1	Small	Onion, minced

DIRECTIONS

Mix all the ingredients together and heat until warm. Serve over chicken or beef.

Simple Sauce for Meat

INGREDIENTS

1/4	Cup	Bacon fat or butter
1	Cup	Chopped onions
1/2	Cup	Tomato puree
1/2	Tsp	Chili powder
1/4	Cup	Worchestershire sauce
1	Tsp	Oregano
3/4	Cup	Water
1/4	Cup	Olive oil
1/4	Cup	Sugar

DIRECTIONS

Melt bacon fat and saute the onions and garlic lightly. Add the rest of the ingredients and simmer for 30 minutes. Serve over meat.

Italian Spaghetti Sauce
I learned how to make this dish from an Italian movie producer in Tahiti

INGREDIENTS

2		Small onions
1/4	Clove	Garlic, crushed
1/4	Cup	Olive oil
1	Tbl	Crushed basil
1	5-oz	Can tomato puree
5	5-oz	Cans water
		Salt and pepper

DIRECTIONS

Put the chopped onions in a saucepan and just cover with olive oil. Over medium heat saute onions until transparent. Add garlic, basil, salt, and pepper. Stir fry for one minute. Add the tomato puree and water. Bring to a boil. Turn heat down and simmer with lid on until garlic is soft. Remove from stove and stir in the rest of olive oil.

Cook spaghetti according to directions on package. When cooked, add 1/2 cup cold water to boiling spaghetti. Drain and add 1 tablespoon butter and stir until spaghetti is coated. Pour a small amount of sauce over the spaghetti and stir. Serve spaghetti with a few tablespoons sauce on top. Sprinkle with parmesan cheese.

Spicy Sauce
Onion soup adds the flavor

INGREDIENTS

2	Tbls	Butter
1	Clove	Garlic, crushed
1	Small	Onion, minced
1/2	Tbl	Sugar
1/2	Tsp	Dry Mustard
1/2	Tsp	Chili powder
1/2	Tbl	Worchestershire sauce
1	Tbl	Parsley
1/2	Tsp	Paprika
1	Can	Onion soup (or 1 package). If dehydrated soup, mix with half the water called for in the directions on package.
1	Tbl	Vinegar

DIRECTIONS

Melt the butter and saute the garlic and onion. Add the rest of the ingredients and simmer for 30 minutes. Serve over pasta, rice, or meat.

Sri Lanka Easy Curry Sauce
Kari is a Tamil word for sauce from northern Sri Lanka

INGREDIENTS

1		Onion
1		Apple
2	Tbls	Cooking oil
1	Tbl	Curry powder
1	Tbl	Flour
1 1/2	Cups	Stock made from cubes
1	Tbl	Chutney
1/4	Cup	Raisins
1/2	Lb	Cooked meat or chicken

DIRECTIONS

Peel and chop onion and apple and fry in oil. Add curry powder, hot or medium, and flour. Fry gently for 1-2 minutes. Blend in stock and bring to a boil. Add chutney and raisins and simmer for 30 minutes. You now have the basic curry sauce.

Dice cooked meat or chicken and add to the sauce. Season with salt and pepper and simmer gently for 5-10 minutes. Serve with boiled rice and mango chutney.

ACCOMPANIMENTS

Raita Sultanas

INGREDIENTS

6	Tbls	Sultanas
1 1/4	Cups	Yogurt
3	Tbls	Castor sugar

DIRECTIONS

Soak the sultanas for 30 minutes and drain. Beat the yogurt until creamy and add the sultanas and sugar.

Pineapple and onion
DIRECTIONS

Slice onions thin and add to pineapple juice with chunks of pineapple.

Curried Egg and Salmon Savory
Serve over rice or on toast

INGREDIENTS

1	Medium	Onion
1	Small	Can salmon
3	Tbls	Flour
3/4	Cup	Butter
3		Hard-boiled eggs
1 1/2	Cups	Milk
1	Tsp	Curry powder

DIRECTIONS

Melt butter in saucepan. Add finely chopped onion and cook until tender. Stir in the flour and curry powder. Add milk gradually and cook for 3 minutes. Add salmon and diced hard-boiled eggs. Warm through but do not reboil. Serve with rice or buttered toast. Serves five.

Soups

There is no need to spend hours boiling stock for delicious soups. Use quick and easy bouillion cubes or packets dissolved in hot water.

Basic White Sauce for Cream Soups
Make this simple sauce and add vegetables

INGREDIENTS

3	Tbls	Butter or margarine
2	Tbls	Flour
1	Tsp	Salt
		Pepper to taste
2	Cups	Milk

DIRECTIONS

Melt butter in a saucepan. Stir in flour and seasoning. Remove from the heat and gradually stir in the milk. Do it slowly to prevent lumps from forming. Return to the heat and stir until sauce is boiling. Turn down the heat and simmer for 1 minute.

VARIATIONS

Almost any vegetable can be turned into a cream soup. You may also add fish, shrimp, chicken, beef, lamb, and so on—the variety is unlimited.

Carrot Soup

INGREDIENTS

1 1/2	Cups	Carrots
	Large	Potato
1/2	Small	Onion
2	Tbls	Butter
		Salt and pepper
		Pinch sugar
1	Tsp	Dried parsley
		Pinch of Chervil
1	Cube	Chicken stock
2	Cups	Boiling water

DIRECTIONS

Grate the carrots, potato, and onions on medium grater. Melt the butter in a large saucepan and add the vegetables. Add salt, pepper, sugar, parsley, and chervil. Cover with lid and cook very slowly on low heat until the vegetables are tender enough to mash. Dissolve the stock cube in boiling water and stir in the mashed vegetables. Bring to a boil and simmer for 15 minutes. Pour soup through a sieve if you want a clear soup.

Cream of Corn Soup
Make the corn mixture, then add to hot, basic white sauce

INGREDIENTS

1	Large can	Kernely corn
4-6	Slices	Bacon
1		Onion, chopped fine
1		Potato, diced
2	Cups	Basic white sauce (see page 161)
		Salt and pepper
		Chopped parsley or croutons

DIRECTIONS

Drain the corn, reserving the liquid. Remove the rind, if any, from the bacon. Fry the bacon and rind until fat becomes transparent. Remove the rind and fry the bacon until crisp. Remove from the pan and crumble. Fry the onion in the bacon fat and add the potatoes. Fry until just slightly browned. Add the corn liquid and simmer until the potatoes are tender.

You can mash the potatoes and onions through a sieve, or leave them in the soup as they are. Return to saucepan and add the corn and bacon. Heat until hot. Then add the basic white sauce. Heat gently. Stir so the soup will not stick to the bottom of the saucepan. Add salt and pepper to taste. Serve hot with chopped parsley garnished or crisp croutons.

Leek and Potato Soup
Use basic white sauce with a leek mixture

INGREDIENTS

3		Leeks
1		Onion
2	Tbls	Butter (heaping)
2	Large	Potatoes
2	Cups	Basic white sauce (see page 161)
		Salt and pepper to taste

DIRECTIONS

Make the basic white sauce and keep warm. Melt the butter in a skillet and add leeks, onions, and potatoes, all chopped very fine. Cook and stir until the onions are transparent. Add just enough water, about 1/4 cup, to the vegetables. Cover with a lid and simmer until the potatoes are tender. Mash, puree, or leave vegetables as they are and pour into the hot basic white sauce. Serve with chopped chives, chopped parsley, or golden croutons.

Canadian Clam Chowder
Makes a complete meal with bread and butter

INGREDIENTS

2	Medium	Onions
2	Tbls	Butter
2	Medium	Potatoes
		Salt and pepper to taste
1/4	Cup	Grated carrots
1/4	Cup	Cooked peas
1	Large can	Minced clams or fresh minced clams, including juice
1	Tbl	Flour (heaping)
1	Large can	Evaporated milk or equivalent

(continued)

DIRECTIONS

Melt the butter in a large saucepan. Saute the chopped onions until transparent. Add the cubed potatoes, salt, pepper, and clam juice from either fresh or canned clams, or water. Boil until potatoes are nearly cooked. Add the carrots. Do not drain. Add the clams and reheat until boiling. Mix flour with a little water and gradually add to the clam mixture. Use only enough flour to make the mixture thick. Stir constantly to prevent sticking and cook for a few minutes. Add the milk slowly and bring to the boiling point, but do not boil. Add the peas. Remove from the heat and set aside for about 10 minutes to marry the flavors. Reheat before serving.

Carrot Soup and Corn Beef
A quick lunch. Just open a few cans

INGREDIENTS

1	Small can	Carrots
1	Tbl	Butter (heaping)
2		Onions, chopped fine
3/4	Cup	Water
1/2	Tsp	Salt
1	Tbl	Flour
2	Tbls	Powdered milk
1	Can	Corn beef

DIRECTIONS

Drain the carrots and mash until pulpy. Put butter into a saucepan and add the onions. Saute until transparent. Add the mashed carrots and 1/4 cup water and simmer until onions are cooked. Mix the salt and flour with a little water to make a paste. Add the paste to the carrot mixture. Stir and simmer until the carrot mixture thickens.

Mix the powdered milk with a little of 1/2 cup of water, until smooth. Then add the rest of the water. Add the milk to the carrot mixture. Stir while adding. Open the corn beef, break it into chunks, and add to the carrot soup. Heat until the meat is hot and then serve.

Carrot and Orange Soup
Carrots and orange with a dash of tabasco

INGREDIENTS

1	Tbl	Butter
1	Cup	Carrots
1	Small	Onion
1	Clove	Garlic, crushed
2	Cups	Water
2		Chicken cubes
		Salt and pepper
1		Orange
1/2	Tsp	Brown sugar
		Few drops tabasco sauce
		Chopped parsley

DIRECTIONS

Melt butter in a heavy saucepan. Add the chopped vegetables and garlic. Turn them in the hot butter to coat them thoroughly. Cover and cook over low heat for 10 minutes. Vegetables will be slightly softened but not colored. Pour in the stock and sprinkle with salt and pepper to taste. Simmer until vegetables are quite soft. Mash with a fork or rub through a sieve.

Return the vegetables to the rinsed out pan and stir in the grated rind and juice from the orange. Reheat the soup and add sugar, tabasco, and more salt and pepper to taste. When hot, serve with chopped parsley garnish.

You can use canned carrots, but drain off the juice before putting them in the butter.

Cheese Chowder
With onion, carrots, and celery

INGREDIENTS

1/2	Cup	Onions, chopped fine
2	Tbls	Butter
1/4	Cup	Flour
2	Cups	Milk
1/2	Cup	Cubed cheese
1 3/4	Cup	Chicken broth
1/4	Cup	Diced carrots
1/4	Cup	Diced celery
		Salt and pepper
	Dash	Paprika

DIRECTIONS

Melt the butter and saute the onions in a saucepan. Add flour, carrots, celery, chicken broth, salt, and pepper. Bring to a boil and simmer until the carrots are cooked. Add milk and heat until almost boiling. Add cheese and stir until cheese is melted. Sprinkle with paprika and serve.

VARIATIONS

Add chunks of diced ham before adding the cheese.

Add sliced frankfurters with cheese, heat.

Add crushed garlic clove and 1/2 teaspoon hot sauce with the first ingredients.

Add 1 small can of undrained shrimp.

Egg Lemon Soup from Turkey
This delightful soup recipe is from a little Turkish fishing village

INGREDIENTS

4		Chicken cubes
1/2	Cup	Uncooked rice
1	Medium	Onion, diced
1	Small	Carrot, diced
		Pepper to taste
	Dash	Cayenne pepper
5	Cups	Water
2	Tbls	Butter (heaping) or margarine
2	Tbls	Flour
2		Egg yolks, beaten
		Juice of 1 large lemon

DIRECTIONS

Put water, chicken cubes, onions, carrots, pepper, cayenne pepper, and rice in a large saucepan. Boil until the vegetables and rice are tender.

In another pan melt butter and add the flour. Add a little of the hot mixture to the melted butter. Pour into the vegetable mixture. Stir and cook until slightly thickened.

In a small bowl beat the egg yolks. **Do not** stop beating while slowly adding the lemon juice. Keep beating and slowly add a little of the hot soup until the eggs are the same temperature as the soup. Do not stir soup. Remove from stove and pour the egg mixture into the soup. Do not stir but shake the pan to mix. Set aside for a few minutes to thicken and then serve.

VARIATIONS

This egg lemon sauce can be added to stews or poured over fish or chicken. Secret: Beat continually and don't stir—shake—into stews or soups.

Cream of Curry Soup

INGREDIENTS

1	Small	Onion
4	Tbls	Butter or substitute
1	Tsp	Curry powder
1	Can	Cream of chicken soup
1		Soup can of water
2	Tsps	Lemon juice

DIRECTIONS

Peel and chop the onion. Melt butter and add the onion and curry powder. Saute until onion is transparent. Stir in the soup and water until well-
blended and heat until just hot. Remove from the stove, add the lemon
juice, and serve.

French Onion Soup

With croutons and grated cheese

INGREDIENTS

3	Large	Onions
3	Tbls	Margarine or butter
1	Tbl	Flour
2	Cups	Milk
		Salt and pepper
3/4	Cup	Grated cheese

DIRECTIONS

Saute sliced onions in butter until transparent, but not brown. Mix in the
flour. Stir while adding the milk and bring to a boil. Simmer for 8 minutes,
or until the onions are tender. Season with salt and lots of pepper. Add
more butter if desired.

Make croutons while soup is cooking. Serve the soup topped with hot
croutons and sprinkled grated cheese.

Curried Potato Soup

INGREDIENTS

2/3	Cups	Finely chopped onions
1	Tsp	Curry powder
2	Tbls	Butter
3	Cups	Diced potatoes
2	Cups	Boiling water
1	Tsp	Salt
2 1/2	Cups	Milk

DIRECTIONS

Melt the butter in a saucepan and add the onions. Saute until they are transparent. Add curry powder. Cook and stir for a few more minutes. Add diced potatoes, boiling water, and salt. Cover with lid and cook until potatoes are tender. Mash the potatoes and add milk. Heat slowly and serve.

Add a little flour mixed with water if you prefer a thicker soup.

Lentil Soup
Creamy with tomato flavor

INGREDIENTS

1	Cup	Lentils
3	Tbls	Olive oil or cooking oil
		Bay leaf
1/2	Tsp	Basil or rosemary
4	Cups	Water
1		Tomato
2	Tbls	Tomato paste
		Salt and pepper

DIRECTIONS

Soak the lentils overnight. Pour off the water and add fresh water. Bring to a boil. Drain off the water again and add fresh water. Add olive oil, bay leaf, sweet basil or rosemary, salt and pepper to taste and bring to a boil. Simmer until the lentils are tender. Add more water if necessary. Add chopped tomato and tomato paste. Season to taste and simmer until soup is creamy. Serve.

Shrimp and Vegetable Chowder
Use canned vegetables and shrimp

INGREDIENTS

1	Can	Mixed vegetables
1	Small	Onion chopped
4	Cups	Cold milk
1/4	Cup	Flour
1	Tsp	Salt
	Dash	Pepper
4 1/2	oz can	Shrimp, drained
1/4	Cup	Butter

DIRECTIONS

Melt the butter in a saucepan and saute the onion until tender. Add the vegetables, salt, and pepper. Mix flour with a little milk and add the balance of the milk to the vegetables. Heat until merely boiling. Then add the flour mixture. Stir to prevent lumping. When thickened, remove from the stove and add the drained shrimp. Let sit for a while to marry the flavors. Reheat before serving. Do not boil.

Rice

Yields of Rice

Regular milled:	1 cup = 3 cups cooked
Parboiled	1 cup = 4 cups cooked
Brown	1 cup = 4 cups cooked
Instant or Precooked	1 cup = 2 cups cooked

Instructions for making perfectly cooked rice

1. Wash rice and put in a saucepan with a lid.

2. Cover the rice with enough water so that if you lay your hand on top of the rice, the water will just cover the fingers. In other words, there should be 1 inch of water above the rice.

3. Put the asbestos pad over the flame on high heat and put the saucepan on top with lid off.

4. When the rice is boiling rapidly, put the lid on and turn off the burner. The rice will cook from the heat in the asbestos pad. Or you can simmer on very low heat for 10 minutes.

5. Rice should be dry and fluffy. If it is still moist, do not stir. Put the lid on and simmer until rice is dry.

Braised Rice Dinner
You can add fish flakes, smoked fish, crab, or lobster

INGREDIENTS

4	Tbls	Cooking oil
4	Cloves	Garlic
1/2	Cup	Onions
2	Cups	Rice
4	Cups	Water
2	Tbls	Chives
1 1/2	Tsps	Chili
2	Tsps	Salt
		Pepper to taste
2	Tbls	Parsley
1	Tsp	Lime or lemon juice

DIRECTIONS

Heat cooking oil in a skillet. When light haze appears, add chopped garlic cloves. Stir fry for 1 minute until lightly browned. Remove from the oil and add chopped onions. Saute for 5 minutes. Pour uncooked rice into the mixture and stir constantly until rice becomes opaque. Add water, chopped chives, choped chili (fresh if possible), salt and pepper to taste. Bring to a boil, reduce the heat, and simmer for 10-15 minutes.

Stir in fish flakes, smoked fish, crab meat, lobster, or whatever you desire. Add chopped parsley, and strained lime or lemon juice and simmer for approximately 5 minutes or until most of the liquid is absorbed.

Rice Dinner for Two
Smoked fish fillets, coconut cream, and curry

INGREDIENTS

1	Small	Onion chopped
1	Clove	Garlic, mashed
1	Tbl	Butter
1	Cup	Uncooked rice
1	Tbl	Hot curry powder
1/2	Tsp	Salt

(continued)

1	Tsp	Chopped parsley
1	Small can	Sliced green beans drained
		Juice from 1/2 lemon or lime
1	Can	Smoked fish fillets
1/2	Cup	Coconut cream
		or 1/2 Cup Milk plus 2 Tbls desiccated coconut

DIRECTIONS

Saute the onion and garlic in butter. Add the rice and stir fry until rice is opaque. Add salt and just cover with water. Bring to a rapid boil. Stir, lower the flame, and cover with lid. Simmer for 15 minutes until rice is tender. Add parsley, fish fillets broken into bite size pieces, drained green beans, and lemon juice. Reheat thoroughly, stirring lightly. When hot, remove from flame and add 1/2 cup coconut cream. Mix slightly and serve.

Peanut Rice
Serve with chicken

INGREDIENTS

2	Cups	Cooked rice
1/2	Cup	Chopped celery
3	Tbls	Butter
1	Tbl	Onion, chopped fine
1/2	Cup	Chopped salted peanuts
		Parsley or chives

DIRECTIONS

Melt butter in a skillet and add the celery. Cook 5-6 minutes until the celery is tender. Add the onion and cook for a further minute. Add the cooked rice and mix in the peanuts. Toss lightly so as not to break down the rice kernels. Serve with a sprinkling of chives or parsley.

Rice Viennese Style
Contains lots of paprika

INGREDIENTS

1	Small	Onion, minced
3	Tbls	Margarine
1	Cup	Uncooked rice
		Salt and pepper
2	Cups	Beef stock
1	Cup	Canned peas, heated
1	Tsp	Paprika

DIRECTIONS

Brown onion lightly in tablespoon of margarine, add rice, and cook until glazed. Season with salt and pepper. Add beef stock and bring to a boil. Turn flame down and simmer until rice is tender. (Stock should be entirely absorbed.) Carefully stir in the peas with a fork. Add 2 tablespoons margarine and sprinkle with paprika. Serves 4-5.

Rissotto

DIRECTIONS

Cook 1 cup uncooked rice and 1/4 cup minced onions in 1/4 cup butter until opaque. Add 2 cups chicken stock, cover, and cook until rice is tender. Add 1/4 cup grated Parmesan cheese and 2 tablespoons butter. Serves 6. Serve with chicken or beef.

Pilaf

DIRECTIONS

Make like rissotto, but don't use the cheese. Season with oregano, basil, or rice seasoning.

Oriental Fried Rice

INGREDIENTS

2	Tbls	Chopped green onions
3	Tbls	Oil
3	Cups	Cooked rice
1	Large	Egg
2	Tsps	Soy sauce
		Chopped almonds

DIRECTIONS

Saute the onions in the oil until wilted. Add white rice and stir fry until rice is hot. Combine the egg and soy sauce and beat slightly. Stir the egg mixture into the hot rice and cook until egg is set. Add chopped almonds to each serving. Serve with chicken, shrimp, or cubed fried beef.

Rice Rings for Salad

Plain Ring

Combine 3 cups hot, cooked rice and 1/4 cup chopped parsley. Press into greased mold ring. Unmold at once onto platter. Fill with creamed tuna or any vegetable-meat combination.

Confetti Ring

Combine large half cup of cooked green peas with 3 cups hot, cooked rice. Add 3 tablespoons chopped pimiento or red pepper, not hot, and 2 tablespoons melted butter. Press into greased mold ring. Unmold at once onto a platter. Fill with creamed fish, cheese, or meat.

East Indian Ring

Heat 2 tablespoons butter in a skillet. Add 3/4 cup chopped onions and 2 tablespoons slivered almonds. Saute until golden. Add 1/4 cup raisins and heat until plump. Add 3 cups hot, cooked rice. Mold in greased ring. Unmold at once onto platter. Fill center with curried meat or vegetables.

Vegetable Dishes

Cauliflower Polonaise

Toasted bread crumbs, green parsley, and egg dress up the most ordinary cauliflower

INGREDIENTS

1	Medium	Cauliflower
1		Hard-boiled egg
3	Tbls	Parsley, finely chopped
2	Tbls	Butter or margarine
		Juice from 1 lemon
3/4	Cup	Soft bread crumbs or 1/3 cup dried bread crumbs

DIRECTIONS

Cook the cauliflower in boiling salted water until just tender. Don't overcook as it will loose its flavor. Drain and put aside. Keep warm. Melt butter in a skillet and add the bread crumbs. Stir constantly until golden brown. Sieve the egg and mix with chopped parsley. Cut the cauliflower into pieces, arrange on a serving dish, and sprinkle the bread crumbs, egg, and parsley mixture over the top. Drizzle with the lemon juice. Serve.

Curried Potatoes
Cold cooked potatoes simmered in curry and chicken broth

INGREDIENTS

3	Cups	Cooked potatoes
1	Small	Onion
1/4	Cup	Butter or margarine
1 1/2	Tsps	Curry powder
1 1/2	Tsps	Lemon juice
1/4	Cup	Chicken broth

DIRECTIONS

Mince onion and saute in butter or margarine until tender. Add cooked, diced potatoes and cook until butter is absorbed. Mix curry powder with lemon juice and add to chicken broth made with hot water and a chicken cube. Sprinkle all over the potatoes and simmer until the mixture is hot. Serves four.

Sour Cream Potato Patties
Cooked potatoes and sour cream

INGREDIENTS

2	Cups	Grated, cooked potatoes
		Salt and pepper
1	Cup	Flour
		Sour cream
		Parsley or chives

DIRECTIONS

Mix the potatoes, salt, and sifted flour together. Add enough sour cream to make a dough stiff enough to be able to roll. Place dough on a floured board and roll to 1/8 inch thickness. Cut into 2-inch rounds with cookie cutter. Fry in butter in a skillet until golden brown. Serve with chopped parsley or chives.

Chinese Style Vegetables
Saucy crisp cooked vegetables with leftover meat

INGREDIENTS

1	Tbl	Oil
2	Cloves	Garlic, mashed
3		Green onions, chop stems
1/2	Cup	Carrots, sliced thin
1/2	Cup	Green beans, cut into strips
2	Cups	Chinese cabbage, chopped; cut white stalks into inch pieces
		Any leftover meat, ham, chicken, or corn beef
1/4	Cup	Water
1	Tbl	Soy sauce
1	Tbl	Corn starch
		Salt and pepper to taste

DIRECTIONS

Heat oil in a skillet until a haze forms. Add the garlic and cook for 2 minutes on lowered heat. Add the carrots and beans and stir until coated with oil. Add 1/4 cup water. Cover with lid and cook gently until vegetables are nearly tender. Add the green onions and white stalks and cook for a few minutes. Mix the corn starch, soy sauce, and water together. Add to the vegetables, stirring constantly. Add the meat pieces and top with the chopped Chinese cabbage greens. Put the lid on and heat until the cabbage is wilted. Toss lightly, adding salt and pepper to taste. Serve with rice. Top with chopped peanuts, sesame seeds, or chopped pineapple.

Eggplant Parmigana

This recip e is from yachtsman we met in Tonga

INGREDIENTS

4-5	Long	Or 3 round eggplants
		Mild cheese (mozarella or cheddar), sliced
1	Large	Onion, sliced
1	Can	Tomato paste or puree
1	Clove	Garlic, mashed
		Oregano
		Salt and pepper
1/4	Tbl	Sliced Salami

DIRECTIONS

If using tomato paste, dilute until it pours. Pour enough tomato puree into a skillet to cover the bottom. Slice eggplant 1/4-inch thick. Alternate layers of eggplant, onion, salami, cheese, and spices. End with cheese on top. Pour the rest of tomato puree over top. Cover and cook until the eggplant is tender. Top layer of eggplant may have to be pushed under the liquid to cook. Eggplant gives off a lot of water but check now and then to be sure there is enough liquid. After the eggplant is cooked, let sit awhile to absorb the juices. The longer the better!

Mediterranean Tomato Bake

Simmer in skillet and serve as a vegetable

INGREDIENTS

3/4	Lb	Tomatoes, skinned and sliced
1	Cup	Onions, peeled and sliced
1	Clove	Garlic
2-3		Green peppers, sliced
		Salt and pepper to taste
		Good dash of oregano
4	Tbls	Olive oil

(continued)

DIRECTIONS

Crush the garlic in a little salt, add to the oil, and add salt and pepper.
Arrange the tomatoes, onions, and green peppers in alternate layers in a skillet. Pour the oil over the vegetables. Cover skillet with lid or foil. Cook slowly
on an asbestos pad over low heat for approximately 30 minutes. The tomatoes will give off enough juice to prevent the vegetables from sticking to the
pan. If sauce is too thin, take lid off and cook for another 5-10 minutes. Serve
with meat and potatoes.

Little Yam Puffs
Looks like little oven roasted potatoes

INGREDIENTS

2	Cups	Raw yams, grated
1		Egg
1	Tbl	Corn starch
2	Tbls	Flour
1/4	Tsp	Baking powder
		Salt and pepper to taste

DIRECTIONS

Mix the above ingredients and let sit for 30 minutes. Form into balls and
deep fry until golden brown. Drain on paper and serve with ham.

Yam Pudding

Yam crust surrounding seasoned meat

INGREDIENTS

3	Cups	Cooked yam
1	Large	Onion, diced
1	Tbl	Butter
1		Tomato
		Salt and pepper to taste
1/2	Lb	Meat or fish, cooked and chunked
1	Cup	Cold water
	Dash	Worchestershire sauce
1	Tbl	Tomato paste

Optional: Add chili, sweet basil, or 1 Tbl white or red wine

DIRECTIONS

Grease a bowl and line it with three-fourths of the mashed yam. Saute the onion in butter, add the chopped tomato, and just heat. Add meat or fish, salt, and pepper. Add water mixed with Worchestershire sauce and tomato paste. Stir just enough to mix them and pour over the yams. Use the rest of the yam for a top crust. Cover the bowl with aluminum foil and steam in a saucepan partially filled with water for 1 hour.